Toolkit Structure and Site Use

Results of a high-power use-wear analysis
of lithic assemblages from Solutré
(Saône-et-Loire), France

William E. Banks

BAR International Series 1970
2009

Published in 2016 by
BAR Publishing, Oxford

BAR International Series 1970

Toolkit Structure and Site Use

ISBN 978 1 4073 0503 5

© W E Banks and the Publisher 2009

The author's moral rights under the 1988 UK Copyright,
Designs and Patents Act are hereby expressly asserted.

All rights reserved. No part of this work may be copied, reproduced, stored,
sold, distributed, scanned, saved in any form of digital format or transmitted
in any form digitally, without the written permission of the Publisher.

BAR Publishing is the trading name of British Archaeological Reports (Oxford) Ltd.
British Archaeological Reports was first incorporated in 1974 to publish the BAR
Series, International and British. In 1992 Hadrian Books Ltd became part of the BAR
group. This volume was originally published by Archaeopress in conjunction with
British Archaeological Reports (Oxford) Ltd / Hadrian Books Ltd, the Series principal
publisher, in 2009. This present volume is published by BAR Publishing, 2016.

Printed in England

PUBLISHING

BAR titles are available from:

BAR Publishing
122 Banbury Rd, Oxford, OX2 7BP, UK
EMAIL info@barpublishing.com
PHONE +44 (0)1865 310431
FAX   +44 (0)1865 316916
       www.barpublishing.com

ABSTRACT

Upper Paleolithic groups used the open-air site of Solutré as a location to intercept and hunt horse and reindeer herds. While it is clear that killing and butchering these animals were the principal site activities, differences in the composition of the recovered lithic assemblages from the different cultural components suggest variability in secondary site activities and lithic tool use over time. High-power use-wear methods are used to evaluate the relative extent of the variability in tool use to test this interpretation. The analysis of high-resolution epoxy casts of sampled artifacts is described, use-wear attributes that function as proxy measures of curation are identified, and temporal differences in secondary site activities and toolkit structure are documented. The use-wear results demonstrate that tool function and typology are closely correlated and do not change over time. The results of statistical evaluations of tool use, use-wear curation signatures, and metric attributes indicate that some time periods are characterized by more versatile curated lithic toolkits than others. Temporal differences in toolkit structure and secondary site activities appear to be the result of changes in mobility and changes in how Solutré was incorporated into subsistence systems during the Upper Paleolithic.

ACKNOWLEDGMENTS

I would like to thank Drs. Anta Montet-White, Marvin Kay, Jean Combier and Ivana Radovanovic for their advice and support.

TABLE OF CONTENTS

Chapter 1: Introduction 1
    Analysis Goals 2
Chapter 2: Site Background 4
    Climate and Solutré Occupations 4
    Stone Tool Assemblages 6
Chapter 3: High-Power Use-Wear Methodology 8
    Background 8
    History 8
    Use-Wear Methodologies 9
    Use-Wear Samples 10
    Casting Methodology 12
    Examination 14
Chapter 4: Experimental Replication 17
    Background 17
    Recorded Use-Wear Attributes 18
    Solutré Experimental Program 20
Chapter 5: Curation and Typology 30
    Curation 30
    Curation Use-Wear Signatures 32
    Typology and Microwear 33
Chapter 6: Database and Wear Feature Coding 36
Chapter 7: Analysis 42
    Chi-Square Comparisons 42
    ANOVA Results 45
    Typology 49
Chapter 8: Summary and Conclusions 51
Appendix A: Experimental Tool List 54
Appendix B: Experimental Photomicrographs 56
References Cited 66

LIST OF FIGURES

Figure 1: Map of Solutré excavation blocks 1
Figure 2: Map of France and general site location 4
Figure 3: Solutré conventional C14 ages 4
Figure 4: Solutré AMS C14 ages 5
Figure 5: Denuziller casting image 1 14
Figure 6: Example of planar orientation variation 14
Figure 7: Denuziller casting image 2 15
Figure 8: M12 Est Au1 WEB 5 – scraping, hard contact 37
Figure 9: L13 WEB 901 – planing 38
Figure 10: P16u14 – burin wear 39
Figure 11: I11u78-487 – burin wear 39
Figure 12: P16u58-198 – burin 2 wear 39
Figure 13: J10 WEB 11 – burin 2 wear 39
Figure 14: P16u68-490 – grooving wear 40
Figure 15: L13hh – cleaning stroke example 41
Figure 16: L13g WEB1 – hafting wear 41
Figure 17: J10u27-2 – prehension 41
Figure 18: L13k WEB18 – butchery wear 43
Figure 19: Use action percentages by time period 43
Figure 20: Hardness percentages by time period 44
Figure 21: Hafting and prehension percentages by time period 44
Figure 22: Edge angle ANOVA by use action and time period 46
Figure 23: Edge angle ANOVA by time period and use action 47
Figure 24: Edge angle ANOVA by hardness and time period 47
Figure 25: Edge angle ANOVA by time period and hardness 48
Figure 26: Edge angle ANOVA of hafted tools 48
Figure 27: Edge angle ANOVA of hand-held tools 48
Figure 28: Natural log normalized width/thickness ratio ANOVA graph 48
Figure 29: Natural log normalized width/thickness ratio ANOVA hafted tools 48
Figure 30: Natural log normalized width/thickness ANOVA hand-held tools 49
Figure 31: I11u88-1708 – Solutrean example of impact and butchery 50
Figure 32: J10u27-1 – Solutrean example of impact and butchery 50

LIST OF TABLES

Table 1: Artifact composition of Use-wear samples 12
Table 2: General use action counts for employable units 42
Table 3: Worked material hardness counts for employable units 44
Table 4: Hafting and prehension wear for employable units 44
Table 5: Degree of edge rounding counts for employable units 45
Table 6: Log normalized width/thickness ratio coefficient of variation 48
Table 7: Employable units' coefficient of variation 49

CHAPTER 1: INTRODUCTION

SOLUTRÉ. The name conjures up many images: President Mitterand climbing "La Roche de Solutré"; the renowned wine Pouilly Fuissé; the type site of the Solutrean cultural complex; the archaeological site where popular opinion long held that prehistoric groups forced tens of thousands of horses to plunge to their deaths off the edge of the cliff during the Upper Paleolithic. This study has nothing do to with politics, wine, or an archaeological misconception, but rather its focus is on the organization and use of the lithic toolkits of the Upper Paleolithic groups that intercepted, killed, and butchered herds of horse and reindeer at Solutré.

The site of Solutré has a long history of archaeological investigation that began in the mid-1800s and continued intermittently until 1998. In 1866, Adrien Arcelin was the first to "discover" the site in that he recognized its importance and archaeological potential. Arcelin and his colleague H. de Ferry began excavations at the site. Years later, Mortillet (1888) based his definition of the Solutrean phase of the Upper Paleolithic on the easily recognizable and well-made Solutrean bifaces recovered from the site's deposits (also see Combier 1976:111). The site underwent numerous excavations during the late 1800s and through the early 1900s. Controlled investigations using modern excavation techniques did not take place until the 1960s and continued periodically through the 1990s. The locations of these excavation blocks are shown in Figure 1.

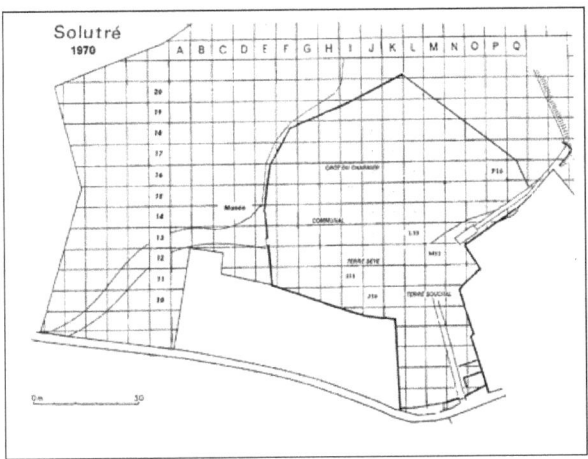

Figure 1: Map of Solutré excavation blocks.

The earliest investigations showed that the site has numerous cultural levels and a complex stratigraphy, but investigators did not fully appreciate this complexity until the mid-twentieth century (Combier 2002a). Modern investigators realized that in order to understand human use of the site, a solid understanding of natural formation processes was critical. In fact, recent analyses have focused on the natural formation and sedimentological characteristics of the site and its deposits (Kervazo and Konik 2002), as well as colluvial site formation processes and the micromorphology of the cultural levels (Sellami 2002). This work has cleared up some issues concerning site formation and climatic conditions and variability (Argant 2002; Jeannet 2002), but the influence of natural formation processes on the archaeological record in some portions of the site still remains unresolved. For example, there is still debate concerning whether the artifact and faunal associations in sector P16 are a result of human action or erosion. The level of faunal articulation and possible pavements (Combier 2002b) and the taphonomic data (Turner 2002) can be interpreted in a variety of ways (Montet-White and Combier 2002). However, recent work in J10 in the Gravettian "magma" (Combier and Hofman 2002; Hofman and Montet-White 1998) has demonstrated that depositional and post-depositional processes have heavily modified the Gravettian bonebed in this portion of the site.

Crucial to the studies introduced above is an accurate understanding of the site's chronology and the timing of human occupation. Numerous radiocarbon ages have been obtained from charcoal and bone throughout recent decades. These ages and more recent AMS ages are synthesized and summarized by Montet-White et al. (2002), and such a summary will prove useful for subsequent site investigations and comparisons with other Upper Paleolithic sites.

Descriptions of the lithic assemblages understandably have a long history in the study of the site. As mentioned above, it was the diagnostic Solutrean bifaces recovered from the site that were used to define this Upper Paleolithic cultural complex. For much of the late nineteenth and twentieth century, lithic studies were predominantly typological in nature. Tool types were classified and used to recognize separate cultural occupations and their distribution across the site. While these studies were detailed and exhaustive and compared the site's lithic assemblages to those from other sites (e.g., Combier 1955; Smith 1966), they were not focused on understanding the technological strategies employed by the groups that used Solutré. Montet-White (2002) summarizes the types (forms) and frequencies of formal tools, informal tools, and debris recovered from the modern excavations and uses the resultant patterns to infer the technological strategies practiced during each of the major time periods. The microwear patterns that form the foundation of this study are used to understand how lithic toolkits were used and infer the activities that took place on site, as well as to recognize changes or consistencies in site activities and tool use throughout the Upper Paleolithic.

For decades, it was thought that the high density of horse skeletal remains in many cultural levels was the result of horses being driven off of the cliff by groups of hunters. This notion was proposed by Arcelin in the early 1870s. Combier (1955) demonstrated that this notion had numerous faults and the data he presented refute the jump hypothesis. Studies since then (Levine 1983; Olsen 1989) numerous faults and the data he presented refute the jump hypothesis. Studies since then (Levine 1983; Olsen 1989) have supported Combier's conclusion. Olsen (1995:66) points out that the jump idea may have persisted for such a long period of time because Combier's (1955) study was published in French and that few archaeologists outside of Western Europe may have had the opportunity to read it.

While these past and recent studies and their inferences have been useful in reconstructing Upper Paleolithic human behavior at Solutré, there are still some issues relating to the lithic assemblages recovered during recent investigations (1960s–1990s) that remain unresolved. For example, in instances where lithic toolkits from different components appear to differ considerably in their composition and/or technology, can one recognize similarities in tool use for specific classes of tools? Do the temporal differences in toolkit composition represent differences in site activities? It is hoped that this use-wear analysis will further refine some of the present inferences and in turn clarify previously unresolved issues. The conclusions reached through the analysis of these use-wear data may also help to precisely focus future research endeavors.

ANALYSIS GOALS

In the next chapter, the characteristics of the lithic assemblages from the different cultural components are discussed. This includes technological descriptions and proposed behavioral inferences for the toolkits recovered from the modern excavations. It will be shown that the behavioral inferences from recent analyses are detailed, we understand the nature of the lithic technology for each of the cultural components, and that these likely represent temporal differences in site activities. These inferences, though, can be subjected to another level of analysis and verification through the use of high-power use-wear methods. The application of high-power use-wear analysis allows one to follow an operational chain to its conclusion and solidify behavioral inferences.

Originally, the term chaîne opératoire (operational chain) described an approach used to investigate the relationship between technology, cognition, and mental templates (Leroi-Gourhan 1964). For the purposes of this study, a chaîne opératoire approach that reconstructs the organization of a lithic technological system at a single site will be used (cf. Sellet 1993:106). The advantage of such an analysis is that it allows one to reconstruct distinct technological strategies through an understanding of the relationships that exist between raw material procurement, tool manufacture, hafting, use, maintenance, and discard (Sellet 1993:107). As will be demonstrated, the earlier stages of an operational chain are not at issue here, but rather the focus is on the patterning observed in the hafting (or lack thereof), use, maintenance, and discard of tools that can be recognized with use-wear analysis, but only hypothesized without it.

At issue here is the need to understand a toolkit's structure and flexibility and the goal of recognizing any temporal variability at Solutré. Schlanger (1994:144) describes this as the study of the relationship between the fixed and the flexible, a concept first introduced by Leroi-Gourhan (1964:164). Also, Schlanger (1990:20) points out that the real existence of a tool is when it is in action or animated by gestures, which is the seminal idea behind the chaîne opératoire. A tool loses its technological meaning as soon as it is removed from its behavioral context. Lithic analyses that are focused on metrics and reduction sequence attributes do not allow one to completely address the issues outlined above. The only methodologies that allow us to take a chaîne opératoire study to its natural completion are those of use-wear analysis. With it, one is able to indirectly witness the tool in action and the gestures of its user.

The primary goal of this study is to conduct a high-power use-wear analysis of a sample of lithic artifacts from each of the Upper Paleolithic cultural components in an effort to address a number of topics. As mentioned earlier, one aim is to test the current inferences of site activities at Solutré. Another issue to be evaluated for each major time period is our understanding of toolkit structure. As will be discussed in the following chapter, some toolkits appear to be highly curated and generalized in function, whereas others appear to be less curated but the tool classes seem to be highly specialized with reference to function and use. The high-power microscopy employed in this study has the ability to test these observations. This analysis attempts to recognize tool curation (see Binford 1973; Bleed 1986; Bousman 1993; Shott 1989) and tool utility (see Kuhn 1994; Shott 1989) and integrate these concepts with the quantification and temporal comparisons of observed wear features.

Use-wear methodologies also allow for the identification of tools in the lithic assemblage that would most likely go unrecognized with only macroscopic examination and typological studies. Such tools would include unretouched blades and flakes that show no signs of use to the naked eye, yet under the microscope have readily identifiable wear features. In addition to unretouched elements, the use-wear results indicate that many assemblages have numerous broken blades and flakes whose breaks were used as ad hoc burins. Such patterns would go unrecognized without microscopic examinations of the artifacts.

Also related to this issue is the ability to identify tools and/or tool classes that were typically hafted rather than hand-held during use, along with the ability to recognize tools that were rejuvenated and/or recycled prior to discard and at what stage of use (early or late) tools were deemed unusable. It will be shown that use-wear methodologies, especially those that consider a range of wear attributes, provide archaeologists with the ability to test and complete analyses of a technological operation chain as it exists at a specific site.

Building upon these issues, another aim of this study is to identify any consistencies and differences in lithic toolkit structure and tool use through time at Solutré. As mentioned earlier, while the primary site function at Solutré was the killing and butchering of large game animals, the lithic assemblage composition for some components suggests that there were possible variations in secondary site function through time. A use-wear analysis allows one to recognize other activities unrelated to or secondarily related to the primary site function. Such methods can also be used to determine if tool use strategies changed or remained stable over time against the backdrop of site function.

If lithic technologies appear to have been used principally the same throughout the Upper Paleolithic, despite obvious differences in assemblage structure, then we may be witnessing cultural reasons for these differences, meaning that different cultures were solving the same problem or similar problems in different ways. However, if there are major differences, what might be the possible reason, or reasons, behind them? While this study and it's relatively narrow focus may not be able to completely answer these questions, it may hopefully serve as a springboard for future lithic technological studies of recovered assemblages in the surrounding region.

CHAPTER 2: SITE BACKGROUND

The site of Solutré is located just west of the city of Mâcon in the hills alongside the Saône River valley (Figure 2). This location places it between the uplands of the Massif Central and the Saône River floodplain. The site is situated immediately below "La Roche de Solutré" which is a small uplift that forms a southerly facing cliff. The archaeological deposits are contained in the talus slope below this uplift of Jurassic limestone. A small stream drainage is situated between the southern side of Solutré and the northern terminus of the Mont de Pouilly which is another, albeit smaller, uplift of Jurassic limestone. This drainage creates a prominent corridor between the two uplifts that served as a natural funnel in which to manipulate the movement of large game animal herds during the Upper Paleolithic. It is interesting to note that a similar geological and geomorphological setting exists between the Solutré cliff and the northerly-situated Rock of Vergisson, but there are no known Upper Paleolithic archaeological deposits in this drainage.

Figure 2: Map of France and general site location.

As was mentioned earlier, early interpretations by Arcelin (1872) suggested that the horses, which make up the bulk of the faunal assemblage, were driven off the Solutré precipice. Later analyses of these animal assemblages by Combier (1955) and Olsen (1989, 1995) concluded rather that the slaughtered animals were driven up against the cliff before being dispatched. The physical nature of the Solutré rock face and the its topography support the conclusions of these faunal analyses. Olsen (1989, 1995) points out that horse herding behavior, their speed, and ability to rapidly change direction would make it essentially impossible for hunters on foot to drive horses up the relatively broad, east-facing slope of the Roche de Solutré uplift to the cliff situated above the site proper. Thus, it is widely accepted that the earlier jump hypothesis is not correct.

CLIMATE AND SOLUTRE OCCUPATIONS

The site's stratigraphy is complex and some cultural components are not present in some site areas, but all major Upper Paleolithic cultural complexes are represented at Solutré. There are numerous occupational gaps in the stratigraphic sequence (Figures 3 and 4), so it is clear that human use of the site was not continuous during the Upper Paleolithic. The conventional and AMS radiocarbon ages from the cultural components correspond closely to interstadial events documented and dated at non-archaeological locales in Europe (La Grande Pile: Woillard 1978; Woillard and Mook 1982; Lac de Bouchet: Reille and de Beaulieu 1988; Les Echets: Beaulieu and Reille 1984, 1989, Reille and Beaulieu 1990:46) and archaeological sites in Western Europe.

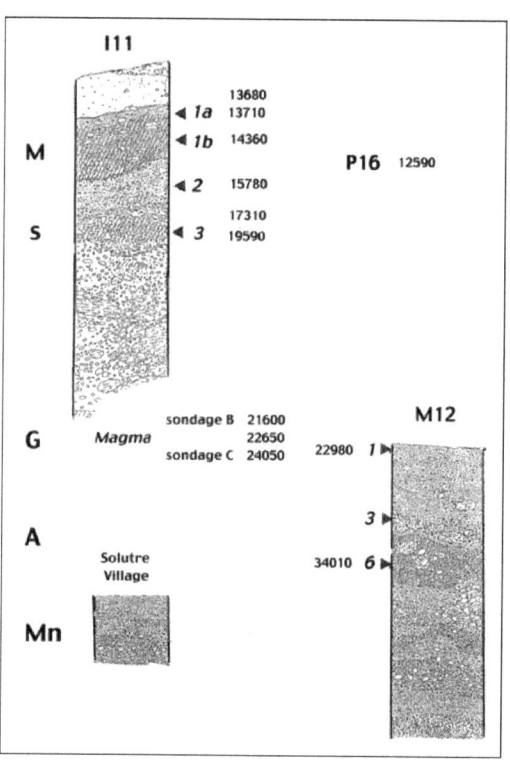

Figure 3: Solutré conventional ^{14}C ages (from Montet-Whte et al. 2002:184).

Aurignacian

The early Aurignacian components at Solutré correspond with the first major climatic amelioration of the Upper Paleolithic termed the Cottés interstadial, which roughly dates to 35,000 yr B.P. and was identified at the site of Les Cottés. This interstadial is dated to 34,770 yr B.P. at the bog site of Tenaghi Philippon in northwestern Greece (van der Hammen et al. 1965; Wijmstra 1969). The Cottés interstadial is followed by a cold episode dated to approximately 33,600 yr B.P. at Arcy-sur-Cure, and 33,300 yr B.P. at Les Cottés. This episode corresponds to the Aurignacian I at the site of Tursac (Leroi-Gourhan 1968).

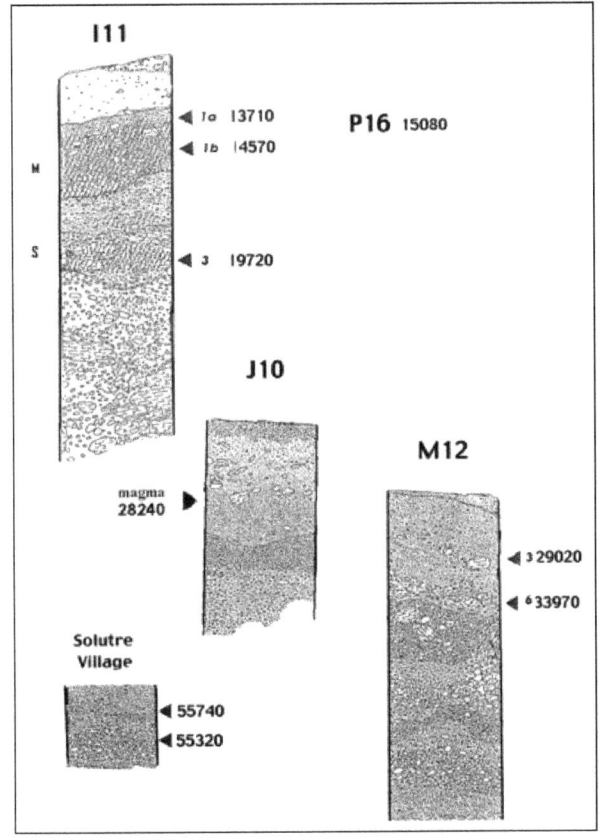

Figure 4: Solutré AMS ^{14}C ages (from Montet-White et al. 2002:185).

The pollen sequence from the Grotte du Renne at Arcy-sur-Cure indicates a warming trend associated with a radiocarbon age of 30,370 yr B.P., which is termed the Arcy interstadial (Leroi-Gourhan 1965) and corresponds to the middle Aurignacian occupation at Arcy. This interstadial corresponds to the Denekamp interstadial in the Netherlands (Donner 1975). The age from La Grande Pile of 29,960 yr B.P. most likely corresponds to this interstadial (Woillard and Mook 1982; also see Leroi-Gourhan 1997). A somewhat earlier age of 32,410 yr B.P. is given at the site of Tenaghi Philippon (Wijmstra 1969).

The Arcy interstadial is also represented at l'abri du Facteur in the Aurignacian II level but is associated with a much younger radiocarbon age of 27,890 yr B.P., which is thought to be too young (Leroi-Gourhan 1968). This climatic event is also seen at Caminade in the Aurignacian II and dated to 29,100 yr B.P. (Paquereau 1978), and at Walou Cave in Belgium at 29,800 yr B.P. (Leroi-Gourhan 1997).

The Arcy interstadial has been correlated to the Stillfried B soil development recognized in central Europe (Klima 1995:42) and dated to 29,940 yr B.P. Damblon (1996) assigns the age range of 31,000–29,700 yr B.P. to the Stillfried B soil. Weissmuller (1997) concludes that the Arcy interstadial and the Stillfried B date to 30,700–30,000 yr B.P. Other sites in central Europe also have soils associated with this climatic amelioration: the Dniestr soil at Molodova V (29,750 yr B.P.); Aurignacian age soils at Dolni Vestonice (29,940 yr B.P.) and Istalosko (30,900 yr B.P.). A pollen analysis from Stranska Skala III shows high percentages of arboreal pollen at 30,980 yr B.P., which Svoboda and Svoboda (1995) point out is a great deviation from the previous tundra environment.

Leroi-Gourhan (1997:157) points out that it is difficult to effectively date the cultural occupations at sites and their specific association with this interstadial because it is composed of three warming events that, combined, span a period of 3000 years without an intervening cold episode. This problem is clearly shown in the range of dates provided above. Nonetheless, the radiocarbon ages associated with the younger Aurignacian occupations at Solutré correspond to the timing of this interstadial documented at other locales.

Gravettian

The Kesselt (oftentimes referred to as the Maisières) interstadial was initially defined on the basis of palynological and sedimentological data from the site of Maisières-Canal in Belgium (Haesaerts and Heinzelin 1979). This interstadial consists of two temperate climatic oscillations and correlates well with the Tenagui Philippon pollen sequence and the Camp Century and Renland ice cores from Greenland (Leroi-Gourhan 1997).

It is difficult to precisely define the duration and exact nature of the Kesselt event because its corresponding time frame (the Gravettian cultural complex) is not well-dated, and with the exception of some central and western European sequences, is almost unknown from a palynological standpoint (Leroi-Gourhan 1997; Weissmuller 1997). A general age range for the event is from 29,000–28,000 yr B.P. Laville (1988) places the event between 29,000–27,800 yr B.P. Weissmuller's (1997) correlations indicate an age range of 29,300–28,600 yr B.P. Such a time range matches well with the Solutré J10 AMS age of 28,240 yr B.P. from the Gravettian magma.

The Tursac interstadial was defined on the palynological study of l'abri du Facteur and is dated there to 23,182 yr B.P. (Leroi-Gourhan 1968, 1997). The other ages for the Tursac are: 24,000–23,000 yr B.P. (Laville 1988:159, Table 8.6), 26,5000–24,500 yr B.P. (Bosselin 1996:191, Figure 10), and 26,000–24,000 yr B.P. (Weissmuller 1997). Another age of 22,980 yr B.P. from the Gravettian "magma" at Solutre corresponds with this interstadial. The Tursac interstadial has also been correlated with the Pavlov soil complex of central Europe assigned an approximate age of 25,000 yr B.P. (Klima 1995). Despite the lack of agreement among the radiocarbon ages, pollen, soil, and sedimentological data from a number of regions point to a marked temperate climatic oscillation (Tursac) after the Arcy interstadial and before the Last Glacial Maximum (LGM). The younger conventional radiocarbon ages from the Gravettian magma at Solutré appear to fall within the Tursac event.

Solutrean

The Last Glacial Maximum was interrupted by two climatic ameliorations. The first is the Laugerie climatic amelioration, which has been dated by a number of researchers. Laville (1988:159, Table 8.6) dates this climatic oscillation to 20,000–18,800 yr B.P., and Bosselin and Djindjian (1988:308, Figure 1) date the end of the Laugerie to 18,800 yr B.P. Weissmuller (1997) suggests a time span between 20,100 yr B.P. and 18,200 yr B.P. for this warming event. At l'abri Fritsch, the Laugerie event is dated to 19,200 yr B.P. The Laugerie oscillation is also evidenced in the pollen sequence from Maisières-Canal in Belgium and is dated to approximately 19,000 yr B.P. (Haesaerts and Bastin 1977; Haesaerts and de Heinzelin 1979; Munaut 1984). In Moravia, the only well-dated site during the LGM is Stranska Skala IV (Svoboda 1990). It has yielded ages of 18,220 and 17,740 yr B.P. (Svoboda 1990). The first date corresponds well with the Laugerie interstadial, while the latter is most likely associated with the Lascaux interstadial.

Two radiocarbon ages of 17,190 yr B.P. and 15,100 yr B.P. are associated with the second amelioration, the Lascaux interstadial, at the site of Lascaux (Leroi-Gourhan and Girard 1979:77). A variety of ages have been provided for this interstadial by other researchers: 17,800–16,500 yr B.P. (Laville 1988:159, Table 8.6), 18,000–16,200 yr B.P. (Bosselin and Djindjian 1988:308, Figure 1), and a beginning age of 17,500 yr B.P. (Weissmuller 1997). The pollen sequence from Maisières-Canal in Belgium also has evidence of the Lascaux interstadial dated to approximately 17,500 yr B.P. (Haesaerts and Bastin 1977; Haesaerts and de Heinzelin 1979; Munaut 1984). This event has also been dated to 17,580 yr B.P. at Tenagui Philippon (Wijmstra 1969). One of the conventional ^{14}C ages from the Solutrean level in sector I11 (17,310 yr B.P.) falls within the Lascaux climatic event.

Magdalenian

After the LGM, climatic conditions remained cold and open herbaceous environments were dominant during the Dryas I. Approximately 13,000 yr B.P., temperatures and humidity increased in Western Europe marking the onset of the Bölling phase in Western Europe (Guiot 1987). The Bölling oscillation marks the beginning of the end of the last Glacial. This phase is characterized by parkland environments with significant stands of pine, hazel, juniper, and oak, and lasted until approximately 12,000 yr B.P. (Straus 1996). The radiocarbon ages from the Magdalenian levels at Solutré are aging materials slightly older than this climatic episode.

The Record at Solutré

The site of Solutré (Saône-et-Loire) is situated near the southern edge of the landscape that was rendered uninhabitable during the Last Glacial Maximum and is in close proximity to the Jura Mountains, which were not occupied during most of the Upper Paleolithic due to severe climatic conditions. Therefore, during much of the Upper Paleolithic, Solutré was situated in a relatively marginal landscape.

The seasonality analyses performed on the faunal material from Solutré indicate that the site was predominantly used during the spring and fall, although animals were also exploited to a more minor degree during summer and winter months during some time periods. Spring and autumn are the seasons when reindeer and horse herds would migrate between the upland summer pastures to the west of the site and the Saône River valley immediately to the east. In many regions of Western Europe (e.g. southern Germany, the Périgord, Gascony: Burke 1993; Enloe 1993; Geneste and Plisson 1993; Pike-Tay and Bricker 1993; Straus 1988; Weniger 1990) during the Upper Paleolithic, the general settlement pattern was occupation and hunting in upland areas during the summer months and wintering in the lowland plains and river valleys. This pattern was a result of large game animal behavior and seasonal movement, as well as resource availability. Thus, it seems that human groups were intercepting horse and reindeer herds at Solutré as the animals moved between winter and summer pastures, and human groups were most likely moving between the upland and lowland regions of their settlement ranges.

It appears that the use of Solutré roughly coincides with interstadial climatic conditions. Even under these climatic and environmental conditions, the region around Solutré most likely was characterized by relatively harsh environmental conditions due to the site's proximity to the Jura Mountains to the east and the uplands to the west.

STONE TOOL ASSEMBLAGES

The lithic assemblages recovered from recent excavations at the site show considerable variation in their composition and organization. This suggests considerable temporal variability in the structure of the toolkits brought to the site and in the types of activities for which these stone tools were used.

The Aurignacian assemblage is relatively lithic poor and shows an economic use of tool stone (Montet-White 2002a). Lithic debris points to the on-site reduction of cores and the production of new tools. Montet-White (2002a) concludes that the rarity of cores and the low frequencies of complete cortical flakes and naturally backed blades point to the introduction of prepared cores to the site. The presence of small flakes is thought to represent core preparation and tool retouch/rejuvenation. Scrapers, strangled blades, and blades with Aurignacian retouch suggest activities other than carcass butchery were performed during this time period. It is possible that activities such as the preparation of hunting and processing tools prior to kills and retooling after kill events are the reasons behind this toolkit patterning.

The Gravettian is characterized by the introduction of prepared cores to the site, and these cores and still usable tools were likely carried away from the site (Montet-White 2002a). It is also not uncommon to find crested blades and crested blade fragments in these cultural levels, both characteristic of core reduction. Formal tools such as scrapers and burins are rare suggesting that the Gravettian components represent the remains of areas devoted to carcass butchery. Additionally, the sampled lithic assemblages are dominated by blades and retouched blades, which is characteristic of butchery having been the dominant activity.

The modern excavations into Solutrean levels at the site are small relative to the other time periods. Nonetheless, a rich and diverse tool assemblage has been recovered (Montet-White 2002a). The Solutrean assemblages include scrapers, edge modified blade and flake tools, burins, and bifacially-retouched points. These bifacially retouched items are characteristic of the Middle Solutrean. Some fragmentary pieces are possibly shouldered Solutrean points, typically associated with the Upper Solutrean, but their fragmentation makes this difficult to evaluate. In all of the Solutrean age levels, there is evidence of lithic reduction, and paired with the presence of hearths and the diversity of the tool assemblage, it has been inferred that camping occupations during this time period were common (Montet-White 2002a). It is reasonable to assume that the use-wear analysis will show these tool assemblages to be highly curated and generalized.

The Magdalenian assemblages from Solutré are diverse in their composition and appear highly specialized. The assemblages recovered from excavation blocks I11 and P16 contain a wide range of tools such as burins, scrapers, unmodified blades and flakes, edge modified blades and flakes, core fragments, core platform rejuvenation flakes, and numerous backed bladelets. The presence of the backed bladelets, the large number of tools assumed to be associated with butchery activities, and the stone pavement feature in P16 thought to represent a processing locale (Combier 2002b) all point to butchery and later animal processing activities to be dominant in this sector of the site. Montet-White (2002b) interprets the arrangements of scrapers and burins in P16 to represent the spatial segregation of hide working areas, burin activities, and animal butchery. The Magdalenian assemblage from I11 is also diverse, but is in a sedimentary context that has been highly reworked by colluvial activities. Thus, the nature of its original archaeological context cannot be known but is likely to have resembled P16 due to the similarities between the two areas' lithic assemblages.

It is necessary to point out that, with the possible exception of sector P16, it is impossible to recognize if the recovered assemblages from the different cultural components represent discrete cultural events at the site. Combier (2002c:76) demonstrates that the Magdalenian component encountered in sector I11 is heavily disturbed and consists of depositional pockets of cultural materials at the base of level 2a. Combier and Hofman (2002) show that the Gravettian age "magma" uncovered in J10 is likely in a completely secondary depositional context. Combier and Montet-White (2002) point out that the cultural materials in the lower Aurignacian levels of sector M12 have a strong orientation counter to the site's slope direction, and that the upper levels appear to have materials randomly oriented on what was once a level surface. In addition to the post-depositional mixing that has occurred, it is important to keep in mind that deposition of the site sediments would have been slow on a human time scale. Therefore, it is highly likely that multiple cultural events took at the site over a long span of time; their material remains would have been incorporated into the same general cultural level, and then likely further mixed by post-depositional conditions. Kervazo and Konik (2002:151) attribute these conditions to a few primary factors. The site is marked by strong relief, and its southeastern exposure made it subject to strong thermal fluctuations. These would have differentially affected the site's different sedimentary layers based on their composition (e.g. plaquettes vs. rounded and weathered limestone fragments). Due to the complex nature of the components' formational histories, one is forced to look at tool use and site activities using broad temporal categories. The factors described above and the low number of lithic artifacts relative to faunal remains would make the results of any comparisons within time periods suspect.

CHAPTER 3: HIGH-POWER USE-WEAR METHODOLOGY

BACKGROUND

The desire to know how prehistoric tools were used, and attempts to understand how they relate to past human behavior, has long been present in archaeological investigations. Behind the practice of classifying and describing these tools, there has always been the desire to understand how tools were used at a moment, or moments, in prehistory and the hope that this would bring us one step closer to understanding prehistoric behavior. One method of reaching this goal has been to examine the surfaces of stone tools for traces of use that can yield clues as to how, and on what materials, they were used. Use-wear analysis has evolved over the decades with archaeology itself. Use-wear analysis, when paired with traditional technological and reduction sequence analyses, allows archaeologists to make detailed interpretations of prehistoric stone tool use, lithic economies, human adaptation, and cultural change.

HISTORY

Use-wear research has been practiced as a form of archaeological investigation in a variety of forms for over a century. In that time, the goals of use-wear analysis, and the questions that it attempts to answer, have remained relatively unchanged, but methodologies have evolved dramatically, as have the variables or data used to answer questions relating to tool use and human behavior. A brief review of the history of use-wear analysis is warranted. This is followed by a review of the two major schools that dominate the discipline today.

Use of Ethnography

The first documented use-wear analysis was undertaken by Nilsson (1838) who examined the edges of stone tools for macroscopic damage or evidence of use. He also used ethnographic analogies to explain what types of activities or tool use could have produced the edge damage that he observed. Evans (1897) employed a similar approach, but Olausson (1980) points out that Evans did not return to his archaeological specimens when making comparisons to the ethnographic data. This early reliance on ethnographic observations to aid in determinations of tool function has continued into recent functional analyses. Gould et al. (1971) used similarities in Australian aborigine tool morphology to make speculations about how Mousterian tools may have been used. A reliance on ethnographic parallels for determining tool function can be faulty, though. Vayson (1922:36) points out that if ethnographic parallels are not combined with examinations of edge wear, incorrect conclusions of tool use could result. Therefore, it is important to keep in mind that identity of form may not correlate with identity of use.

Experimentation

Experimentation has long been an important aspect of use-wear studies (Sehested 1884; Spurrel 1884). Early experimentation programs, much like modern ones, attempted to reproduce the wear patterns observed on archaeological specimens. Curwen (1930) incorporated two innovative aspects that are commonplace in modern experimentation programs: photography and documentation of the length of time that a tool was used. The time that an experimental tool is used has long been recognized as an important variable to record (Crabtree and Davis 1968; Kantman 1971; Sonnenfeld 1962). Keller (1966) advocated the measurement of the number of strokes rather than simply the time used. This can provide a more accurate assessment of edge damage and polish development, but can be extremely tedious.

Experimentation was also used to demonstrate that the wear observed on prehistoric tools was not always cultural in origin (Moir 1914; Warren 1914). The realization that non-cultural actions can produce wear traces is still an important component of modern use-wear studies. Levi-Sala (1986) demonstrated through experimentation that natural processes can leave wear traces on tools that closely resemble, and in some cases are identical to, culturally generated wear traces. She cautioned use-wear analysts not to ignore the possibility that wear features observed on archaeological specimens might be natural in their origin. Such caution and awareness of formational criteria are important aspects of middle range research because archaeologists must demonstrate that wear patterns are not natural in origin before they can be used to make inferences about prehistoric human behavior. This awareness is proving important in the evaluation of possible Pre-Clovis age sites or components in North American where there is some question whether the recovered artifacts were humanly produced and used [e.g., Topper Site (M. Kay 2002, personal communication), Big Eddy Site (Kay 2000)]. Use-wear methods may prove to be central in answering these questions, but the analysts must also assume from the beginning that the wear features are not cultural until their attributes and relationship to the suite of recorded features and tool attributes are shown to be culturally produced.

Semenov (1964) is well known for his use of experimentation. His interpretations were well founded since they were based on an experimentation program that controlled for a large number of variables. Experimentation programs undertaken by Keller (1966), Ranere (1975), and Tringham et al. (1974) were similar in that they attempted to control for a wide range of factors so that more accurate inferences of prehistoric tool use could be made.

It is clear that use-wear analyses risk being meaningless if they are not done in conjunction with an experimental program. The interpretive power of an experimental program can be increased if it is integrated into a larger experimental database. The results of this analysis' experimental program, which were combined with the experimental database at the University of Arkansas, are described in Chapter 4.

Magnification

Olausson (1980:56) points out that there is no chronological pattern in the amount of magnification that researchers have used to identify usewear on prehistoric and experimental implements. According to Olausson (1980), the first published use of magnification in locating usewear was by Quente, in 1914, who employed a magnifying glass. Semenov systematically employed a microscope to study microwear at both low and high magnifications. Low-power microwear analysis employs magnifications up to 100X and is advocated by Odell (1975) and Tringham et al. (1974). High-power microwear analysis employs magnifications that range from 100X to 500X and is focused on the identification of polishes (e.g. Keeley 1974a, 1980; Keeley and Newcomer 1977).

Goals of Use-Wear Analysis

At its most basic level, use-wear analysis attempts to reconstruct how a tool was used. The analysis of a single tool, though, does not contribute much except an interesting snapshot of prehistoric behavior. Lithic technologists are not satisfied with "just-so stories", but rather hope to construct theories of human behavior and decision making as they relate to stone tool technology. Therefore, use-wear studies, while built upon the analyses of individual tools, are ultimately focused on lithic toolkits. By conducting wear analyses on a tool assemblage, the archaeologist hopes to understand how the stone tool technology was incorporated into the economic activities of a prehistoric group or culture (Keeley 1974b, 1980). This is done by interpreting how specific stone tools were used and how individual tool classes functioned within the broader toolkit.

USE-WEAR METHODOLOGIES

The interpretation of tool use and tool function has relied on two principal methodologies with much debate as to which methodology allows for the best inferences of prehistoric human behavior and adaptation as they relate to lithic technology. Use-wear analyses can be divided into one of two broad categories: those that identify and interpret wear features at low magnifications (< 100X), and those that utilize higher magnifications (typically 100X–500X). Each of these methodologies has advantages and disadvantages.

The Low-Power Approach

Practitioners of the low-power approach rely principally on edge damage and the analysis of microflake scar attributes to make determinations of tool use and worked material (Frison 1968; Odell 1975; Odell and Odell-Vereecken 1980; Prost 1993; Tringham et al. 1974; Wilmsen 1968). Striations and well-developed polishes (both additive and abrasive) are sometimes visible and the locations of these features on a tool are evaluated along with the observed edge damage. Low-power studies are conducted with the use of stereomicroscopes and outside light sources and usually use magnifications ranging from 10X–100X.

The low-power approach has the advantage of allowing large samples of artifacts to be analyzed (sometimes entire excavated assemblages) in a relatively short amount of time. The stereomicroscopes needed to perform such an analysis are inexpensive and readily available. Stereomicroscopes also have the advantage of allowing the analyst to view a three-dimensional image of the tool surface, and they have a good depth of field in their optimal range of magnification. Despite these advantages, stereomicroscopes do have a significant loss of resolution at magnifications above 50X and have poor light-gathering capabilities (Keeley 1980:2). The equipment's limitations restrict the flexibility to view use-wear attributes accurately from a wide range of magnifications.

In addition to the failings of the stereomicroscope, the low-power approach has numerous disadvantages. One of the most critical limitations is that the low-power approach is not effective in identifying tools that did not suffer any edge damage during use. Symens (1986) noted that many unretouched blades in her archaeological sample displayed traces of use at high magnifications but did not reveal any signs of use at lower magnifications. The inability of the low-power approach to identify these components of the prehistoric toolkit can seriously hinder the accuracy of any inferences pertaining to the structure and use of a stone tool technology.

A strict reliance on edge damage oftentimes will not allow for an analyst to identify a sequence of uses on different classes of worked materials with a single tool. On a single tool edge used multiple times on different worked materials, only the last period of tool use will be readily visible on the edge. It is difficult, if not impossible, to interpret a sequence of tool use in such a scenario with a low-power approach. For example, if a tool edge were used to process a hard material (e.g., antler) after having been used to process a soft material (e.g., hide), any edge damage associated with the hide work would be overlain or removed by the damage resulting from the antler processing.

Another limitation with a focus on edge damage is that it can be difficult to determine if it is the result of purposeful retouch or actual tool use. Plew and Woods (1985) demonstrated through experimentation and low-power examination of used and unused biface replicas that the form and degree of edge damage could not be used to effectively differentiate between these two possible sources of edge damage.

Finally, the process of edge damage is progressive. Tringham et al. (1974), along with others, note that a brief-episode of use on a material of medium hardness can produce edge damage that resembles damage resulting from longer-term use on a soft material. Such ambiguity oftentimes forces a low-power analyst to make incorrect or broad determinations of tool use. Related to this is the differentiation between edge damage resulting from use and that resulting from purposeful retouch of a tool edge. Minor retouch to an edge with an antler billet can resemble the edge damage associated with scraping use on medium to hard materials. It is virtually impossible to distinguish between these two activities with low-power methods.

The High-Power Approach

High-power methodologies have been used extensively by researchers in Western Europe and the United States and have focused on the identification and interpretation of use-generated polishes. This approach was sparked by the research carried out and described by Semenov (1964). Semenov's research described the "traceology" or kinematics related to tool use and accomplished this through an analysis of striations, edge damage, and abrasive polishes. It is important to incorporate these concepts into a use-wear program since these types of attributes are critical in determining the mechanics of tool use, and to a lesser degree the type of worked material. Subsequent high-power use-wear studies have relied on use-generated polishes and, to a lesser degree, striations to make determinations of tool use and worked material (Keeley 1980). Experimentation has demonstrated that the morphology or surface characteristics and reflectivity of use-generated polishes are highly correlated to the type of worked material (Cook and Dumont 1987; Keeley 1978, 1980, 1981). Polishes, unlike edge damage, tend not to vary according to the manner of tools use.

One methodological problem has been a strict reliance on polish brightness and appearance with little effort to quantitatively describe a polish (e.g. Keeley 1974b:331). A primary criticism of high-power studies has been the subjective nature of polish descriptions (Grace et al. 1987) that are difficult to independently verify. Blind tests have suggested that a strict reliance on polish appearance does not produce a high degree of accuracy in determining the type of worked material (Holley and Del Bene 1981; Newcomer and Keeley 1979; Newcomer et al. 1986). Blind tests demonstrated that an analysis of tool use and worked material should not rely simply on one type of use-wear attribute, and this idea is indirectly suggested by Holley and Del Bene (1981:346) when they questioned whether or not Keeley's determinations were really based on the interpretation of a suite of attributes rather than polish characteristics alone.

Presently, some researchers (Dale Hudler, personal communication 2003) are switching to digital cameras to document features. These cameras are used in conjunction with software packages that allow many attributes to be measured and quantified in a variety of ways. Such a trend may help to alleviate some of the quantification problems that have plagued high-power approaches.

Integration of the Two Approaches

Low-power and high-power use-wear methodologies each have advantages and disadvantages. Fortunately, these two approaches are no longer mutually exclusive, as was the case during the late 1970s and 1980s, because use-wear analysts now see the importance of using all available data for inferring both tool use and function (e.g., Grace 1993, 1996; Unger-Hamilton 1989). Odell (2001:50) points out that it is accurate to view low and high-power methods as strategies that complement each other rather than viewing them as competing techniques. A combination of the two approaches allows an analysis to profit from each approach's advantages while minimizing or overcoming the disadvantages. The combination of low and high-power methodologies and the integration of multiple use-related features are well documented in the literature (Hurcombe 1988; Kay 1996; Keeley 1980; Vaughan 1985). Brink (1978:371) urges the, "... full consideration of all use-wear processes, and an appreciation of their interrelated nature." By themselves, low- and high-power approaches are limited by a number of disadvantages, however when combined, these can be overcome and the advantages of each approach combine to result in more accurate inferences of worked material and tool use. For example, one can see if the attributes observed at high magnifications tell the same story as those traditionally viewed at lower magnifications. Oftentimes, the attributes of the polishes visible at higher magnifications help to more precisely infer what actions and worked materials created the features visible at lower magnifications. Plew and Woods (1985) found that, at low magnifications, it was difficult to distinguish between use-generated edge modifications and technological modifications (i.e., purposeful retouch). Their finding adds support to the argument that high-power techniques should be part of any use-wear analysis since they overcome the difficulties they encountered. Most importantly, if one can find concordance between the attributes viewed at high and low magnifications, then the inferred tool use can be considered more solid than if based solely on observations at a single level of magnification.

The need to focus on a variety of wear features has also been noted in studies that have attempted to quantify polishes at higher magnifications. For example, Gonzalez-Urquijo and Ibanez-Estevez (2003:488) state that a reliance on polish texture and pattern alone is not sufficient for inferring use and worked material accurately. Rather, the collective examination of polish, edge damage, edge rounding, striations, and polish location is necessary (Gonzalez-Urquijo and Ibanez-Estevez 2003:488).

USE-WEAR SAMPLES

One of the primary reasons behind sampling the lithic assemblages for microscopic examination was the existence of transportation restrictions on the archaeological collections that prevented the entire assemblage from being examined with the microscope and optical equipment described below. This and other reasons led to the determination that casting a sample of artifacts from each of the cultural components excavated during the last few decades was the best solution.

It is important to state that each cultural component is viewed as a whole since slow deposition of sediments and post-depositional processes make it impossible to recognize individual kill and butchery events. The site is located in the deposits of a colluvial slope situated immediately below the Solutré precipice, therefore slow deposition rates, colluvial processes, and other postdepositional processes have made it impossible, with few exceptions (P16 excavation block), to recognize individual kill events or site occupations. Hilton (2003) has demonstrated that freeze-thaw episodes in open-air settings, over a three-year time period, resulted in an average artifact movement of over 30 centimeters. When one considers the time depths of even a single cultural component at Solutré, it is clear that postdepositional processes would have essentially blurred the distinctions between individual events. The slow rates of deposition also make the identification of individual events suspect since it is highly likely that multiple site occupations would be combined in a single cultural level. Nonetheless, there appears to be only rare instances of mixing between cultural components because in most areas of the site thick levels of sterile sediment separate them.

In some instances, it has been argued that individual occupation events are distinguishable at Solutré. Combier (2002b) argues that the materials and features uncovered in block P16 represent the relatively undisturbed remains of a single occupation or a few temporally closely spaced cultural events. Turner (2002) on the other hand sees quite a bit of taphonomic evidence to suggest that natural processes have heavily disturbed the cultural materials in block P16. If one accepts Combier's interpretation, then P16 represents an exception to the rule, since it is clear in other site areas that the cultural levels have been extensively modified over time (Combier and Hofman 2002). Block P16 aside, for the site as a whole, the combination of high levels of post-depositional disturbance, small excavation areas investigated in the latter part of the 20th century, and relatively low lithic counts, makes fine-scale analyses of toolkit structure and use impossible or, if attempted, highly suspect. It is for these reasons that there are no stratigraphically distinct use-wear samples within each cultural component.

The first step in the sampling process was to view the entire assemblage from a cultural component in its entirety and items that were heavily patinated or extensively covered with carbonates were eliminated. Extensive patination physically alters the surface of the artifact and in turn destroys microscopic traces of use. Also, it is difficult to remove dense and extensive deposits of carbonates from an artifact's surface with an ultrasonic cleaner. Acid and base solutions can be used to remove carbonates, but one also risks altering the surface of the artifact, and any wear traces, during such procedures. While all artifacts from the site are patinated, the majority of this patination is not heavily developed, and a preliminary use-wear analysis conducted in 2001 demonstrated that light–moderate patination has not adversely affected the microscopic traces of use on most artifacts from the site. A previous examination of the Aurignacian sample (Banks 2002a) demonstrated that animal and human trampling, and postdepositional processes, have not adversely affected wear traces. Examinations of the remaining samples have shown that none of the use-wear samples have been compromised by such factors.

After the removal of heavily patinated and carbonate covered specimens, each assemblage was typologically coded using the typology developed by de Sonneville-Bordes and Perrot (1953), along with additional codes developed by A. Montet-White and myself. These latter codes are: 100 – blade; 101 – edge modified blade; 300 – flake; 301 – edge modified flake; 220 – crest blade or burin spall. Once coded, each assemblage was divided into formal tool, blade, and flake categories. The blade and flake categories include both edge-modified and unretouched elements. Items from these categories were chosen for the use-wear analysis with consideration given to completeness and size. This was done so that the use-wear analysis could effectively evaluate factors related to hafting and prehension. Blades and flakes lacking visible signs of retouch were included to prevent informal and expedient tools from being excluded from the sample (cf. Symens 1986). The operating assumption is that lithic technology and tool use cannot be thoroughly evaluated if the use-wear analysis only focuses on formal tool types along with blades and flakes exhibiting formal and regular retouch. Burin spalls and tool edges removed via burination were also included because they have the potential of exhibiting traces of tool use created prior to tool rejuvenation.

The final samples sorted by time period and artifact class are contained in Table 1. One notes that the sample sizes are not all equal, and this is due to a number of factors. The frequency of lithic artifacts in the modern excavated assemblages varies greatly. The Aurignacian and Solutrean assemblages are relatively lithic poor, while the Gravettian and Magdalenian assemblages have relatively high numbers of lithic artifacts. So recovered sample sizes were the first limitation on use-wear sample sizes. Add to this the fact that heavily carbonated and patinated artifacts were not chosen due to the high likelihood that any wear traces on such specimens had been compromised. Finally, the fact that it would have been prohibitively expensive to cast every artifact led to the selection of pieces that were complete or nearly complete.

Table 1: Artifact composition of Use-wear Samples

Type	Aurignacian	Gravettian	Solutrean	Magdalenian	Total
Formal tools	14	4	12	25	55
Blades	25	38	5	23	91
Flakes	1	2	8	7	18
Total	40	44	25	55	164

While the sample sizes do vary, each time period's sample has a wide range of tool types and is assumed to be representative samples of the recovered assemblages. One will note that relatively few items compose the Solutrean sample, but this is due to the fact that relatively narrow "windows" were excavated into deposits of this age during recent times. Also, when viewed against the large number of lithics in total assemblage, the Magdalenian sample might seem small until one notes that a high percentage of the volume of materials recovered from Magdalenian levels were broken pieces and reduction waste materials (Combier and Montet-White 2002).

CASTING METHODOLOGY

Two major obstacles were encountered while carrying out a use-wear examination of the lithics from Solutré. First, the archaeological collections are curated at the Musée de Préhistoire in Solutré and could not be transported out of France. It was not practical, much less feasible, to transport the needed microscope and photographic equipment to France. Therefore, a method was needed such that replicas of the archaeological specimens could be transported to microscope equipment in the United States—equipment that was suitable for the type of analysis I wished to conduct, and equipment to which I had access. In consultation with Dr. Marvin Kay and Dr. Peter Ungar of the University of Arkansas, I determined that making epoxy casts produced from silicon molds of the sampled archaeological materials was the most effective way of bringing the artifacts to the immobile microscope equipment. Some preliminary casting tests were performed to evaluate how effective the casting methodology was in replicating use-wear features present on the archaeological specimens. Banks and Kay (2003) discuss the casting process and evaluation of the replication efficacy in detail. An abbreviated discussion is provided below.

In contrast to making peels of a stone artifact surface that result in a negative impression, or mold, similar to conventional casting (Beyries 1981; Knutsson and Hope 1984; Moss 1983; Plisson 1983), I produced true or positive casts that were examined microscopically. Bienenfeld (1995) describes a similar casting method. My methods differ in important respects. First, bubbles were largely eliminated in cast production. Problems associated with the long-term integrity of the artifact molds used to make the epoxy casts were overcome. My methods also allow for color control when producing the casts. The casting process employs materials and methods first adopted by paleoanthropologists for scanning electron microscopy that demonstrated a high level of utility for the study of dentition (Rose 1983; Teaford and Oyen 1989; Ungar 1994). With only slight but significant modifications, my casts showed an equally useful application for stone tool use-wear analysis.

Before casting, artifact surfaces were cleaned of any adhering sediment and oils. The most practical method is to place an artifact in a clean polyethylene plastic bag filled with a solution of water and ammonium-based liquid detergent, and then ultrasonically clean it for at least 30 minutes. This method is effective, requires minimal equipment, and the appropriate cleaning solutions are readily available. Of course other cleaning methods are available (e.g. soaking in diluted solutions of HCL or NaOH), but these are much less practical since they employ corrosive or caustic solutions that must be used with caution and can alter the surface of the artifact if used incorrectly. The tools discussed in this study were cleaned with the ultrasonic method.

The production of the mold required a polyvinylsiloxane gel manufactured by Coltène-Whaledent named "President Plus Jet Regular Body." It comes in paired 48 ml tubes from which the gel can be extruded with a 3M Express Vinyl Polysiloxane Impression Material Introductory System that looks and works like a small grease or caulking gun. The gel reproduces features visible up to 10,000X magnification (P. Ungar 1997, personal communication) and maintains its integrity indefinitely (Coltène-Whaledent polyvinylsiloxane gel literature) unless there is sustained exposure to ultraviolet (UV) radiation (D. Burnham 1999, personal communication).

An amount of the polyvinylsiloxane gel sufficient to cover an artifact surface is extruded onto an index card or piece of paper. The hand-held artifact is then pushed into the gel and simultaneously wiggled back and forth to ensure that no air bubbles are introduced into the mold while at the same time producing a mold of the tool edge(s) and adjacent surface(s). The polyvinylsiloxane gel should harden for three to four minutes, after which time the artifact can be removed. The mold is then labeled, placed in a clear polyethylene plastic curation bag, and when not being used to make a positive cast, stored in a UV-safe sealed container.

To make the positive cast, a mixture, described next, of epoxy, epoxy hardener, and pigment concentrate is slowly poured into the mold, so that air bubbles are not introduced or trapped in the epoxy mixture.

Although other brands are available, Tap Plastic's "Four to One Super Hard" that includes the epoxy, a hardener, and pigment concentrate was used for this study. Tap Plastic specifies a four-to-one mixture of epoxy to hardener to which may be added a small amount of pigment concentrate, if desired. Through a trial and error process to eliminate air bubbles from the cast surface which confound analysis, the ideal mixture was determined to be three parts epoxy to one part hardener. When care is exercised, one can keep air bubbles from entering the mixture while pouring it into the mold, thus eliminating the need for vacuum evacuation. For analytical reasons, a brown pigment concentrate is mixed with the epoxy-hardener mixture until it becomes opaque. This pigment produces casts that are of optimal color for viewing under the microscope because they are not reflective. The epoxy casts along with the molds are then safeguarded against prolonged UV exposure and possible damage.

In most cases, the casting process targets an artifact's ventral surface and edges because the ventral surface is typically flat, more likely to have been the leading surface of the tool in direct contact with a worked material and/or haft element, and more easily manipulated for observation under the microscope. Artifact edges are also targeted because they represent the working component of a tool. The combination of a tool's edges and ventral surface on a cast increase the likelihood that wear features associated with tool use will be observed during analysis. However, in some instances, dorsal surfaces were cast. This was done if the artifact's ventral surface was covered extensively by carbonates, appeared to have undergone less silica dissolution than the ventral surface, or if it was hypothesized that an analysis of the dorsal surface, along with the ventral surface, might allow for a more accurate assessment of tool use. Unless otherwise noted, use-wear features were observed on the cast of an artifact's ventral surface.

Replicative Tests of Casting Methodology

To demonstrate that the casting method is accurate in replicating microscopic wear features on archaeological specimens from Solutré, a number of archaeological lithic tools were first examined with the microscope and representative wear features were recorded and photo-documented. These same specimens were cast using the above-described methodology, and the casts were examined in an attempt to relocate and document the same use-wear features recorded on the original items. Two of these casting experiments are described below.

To illustrate, the comparative use-wear results of two patinated and unifacially retouched Mousterian stone tools are presented. The patina present on this study's sample has not resulted in significant silica dissolution that would adversely affect wear features. The patina present on these artifacts is consistent with the patina observed on the majority of tools from the Upper Paleolithic components in the site proper. The two artifacts are part of a Middle Paleolithic collection dated to approximately 55,000 ^{14}C BP from the village of Solutré (Saône-et-Loire), France (Montet-White et al. 2002; Pautrat and Pugh 2002).

The first artifact used in the casting comparison is the medial segment of a steeply retouched sidescraper with a distal snap break (Figure 5). The proximal end has a transverse break about which are wear traces on the ventral surface. These show up reasonably well on the actual artifact (Figure 5a) but are better expressed on the cast (Figure 5b). Variation in image quality is due to slight differences in the microscope stage planar orientation of the artifact and its cast, as well as to deliberate control of cast surface color. The observed details associated with a wear feature can vary greatly based on the planar orientation of an artifact, or cast, under the microscope. This is a product of the microscope type and the Nomarski optics. Therefore, variability in orientation between the original artifact and the epoxy cast explains why slight differences exist in wear feature details between the photomicrographs. Nevertheless, the suite of wear feature attributes needed to infer tool motion and worked material are identical between the tool and its epoxy cast despite slight differences in their expression. Additionally, because color could be controlled for the epoxy cast, the analyzed surface is not highly reflective, thus allowing for a higher resolution of wear feature details. This increased resolution decreases wear feature ambiguity, thereby allowing more detailed and accurate inferences of tool motion and worked material to be made than would be possible on the original artifact.

Differences in the expression of wear feature attributes due to variation in the planar orientation of an artifact under the microscope are further illustrated in Figure 6. These photomicrographs document the same cutting wear feature at the tip of a prismatic blade recovered from Ain Abu Nekheileh, Jordan (Henry et al. 2001). The two photomicrographs were taken on separate days, and after the specimen had been repositioned on a microscope slide plate. Although an attempt was made to faithfully place the artifact on the slide plate in the same manner as before, it was not possible to exactly replicate its previous planar orientation. As can be readily seen, a slight change in planar orientation can dramatically affect the visual expression of wear feature attributes. However, despite the difference in expression, the interpretation of use is not materially affected.

The second Mousterian tool is a naturally backed sidescraper opposite the retouched edge. Wear traces are located on the ventral surface along the naturally backed edge rather than the retouched edge (Figure 7). Other than slight differences that are a result of variation in planar orientation between the artifact and cast, the two images of the wear feature have nearly identical wear attributes and clarity of detail.

'The sample used in this study is small. It is a result of limitations that prevented a large sample of artifacts from being transported out of France while the viability of applying the casting methodology was being evaluated. Since that time, other replication accuracy evaluations have been performed on experimental tools and other archaeological specimens, and support the findings described above. A large sample of artifact casts was evaluated for this dissertation and during those analyses wear features were observed that had the same clarity of detail as those observed on archaeological specimens and

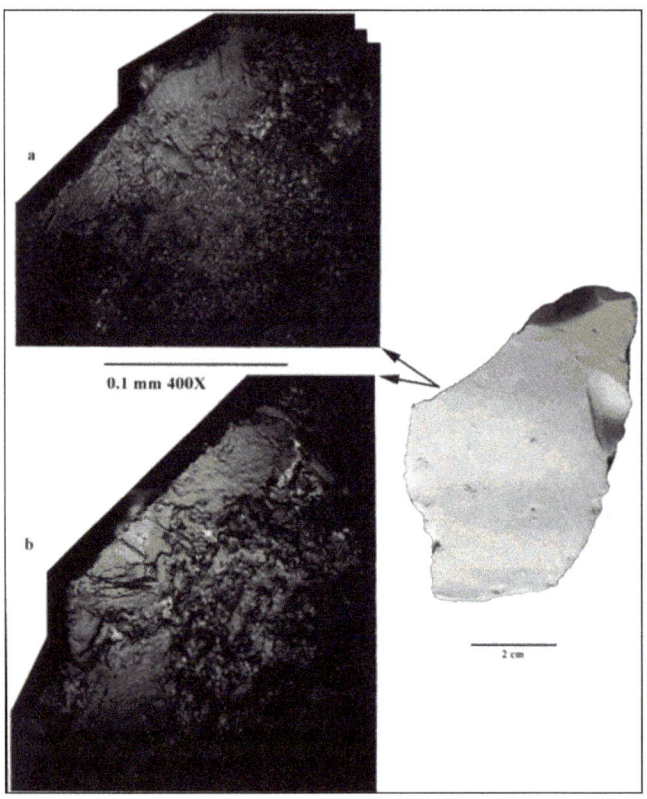

Figure 5: Denuziller casting image 1.

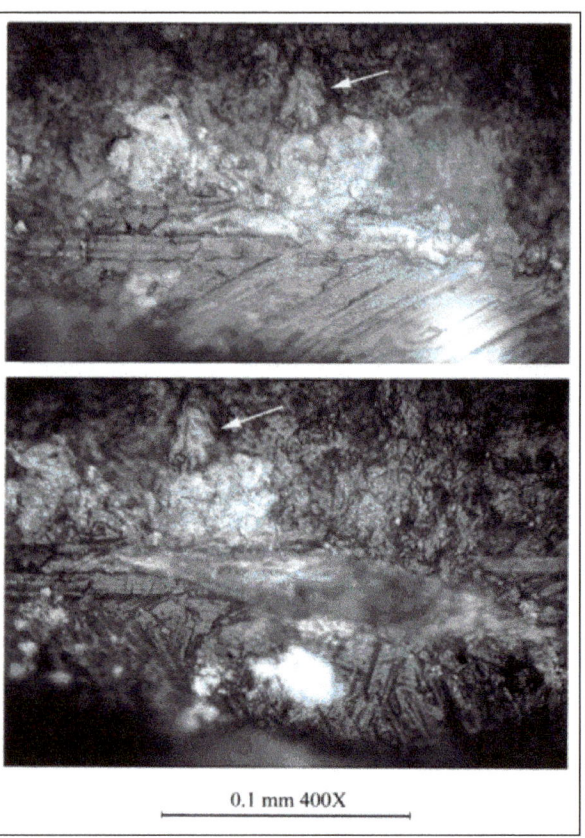

Figure 6: Example of planar orientation variation.

documented in the literature. This correspondence between published features, unpublished but well-documented features, and the large Solutré cast sample provides additional evidence that the casting methodology can accurately replicate wear features on experimental tools and patinated artifacts.

EXAMINATION

This analysis employed a binocular differential-interference microscope with polarized reflected-light and Nomarski optics (Hoffman and Gross 1970) at intermediate range magnifications (100X–400X) for artifact examinations. This microscope is ideal for use-wear studies because it affords a high resolution, three-dimensional view of microtopography far superior to conventional binocular microscopes commonly used to examine wear traces (for examples see: Kay 1996, 1997, 1998).

The ability to view surface features in three dimensions is not possible with incident or reflected-light microscopes equipped with standard optics. It is the Nomarski optics that allow for the high definition views of an artifact's surface topography. Nomarski illumination or Differential Interference Contrast (DIC reflected) is a technique that uses interference of the light illuminating the artifact surface to view surface detail in three dimensions. Polarized light from the illuminator passes through a Nomarski prism that divides the light into extraordinary and ordinary waves. These light divisions then travel through the optic to the artifact surface very close to one another. These orthogonally polarized and parallel light rays illuminate the artifact surface, and any variations in the microtopography of the artifact surface deform the waves of the light rays slightly. These deformed rays are reflected by the artifact surface back through the microscope objective and the Nomarski prism where they are reunited, but in different phases, thus producing a contrast-rich image. This high-definition image can be adjusted with an analyzer that can be manipulated to select or change the specific plane of polarization thereby allowing the small deformations of the light rays or differences in the optical path to be seen as changes in color or intensity. It is oftentimes necessary to change the plane of polarization so that the attributes of a wear feature are visible. Since artifact surfaces are rarely flat on a microscopic scale, a single plane of polarization may not be adequate for locating and viewing every feature present on an artifact, and thus must be adjusted numerous times during the examination of an item.

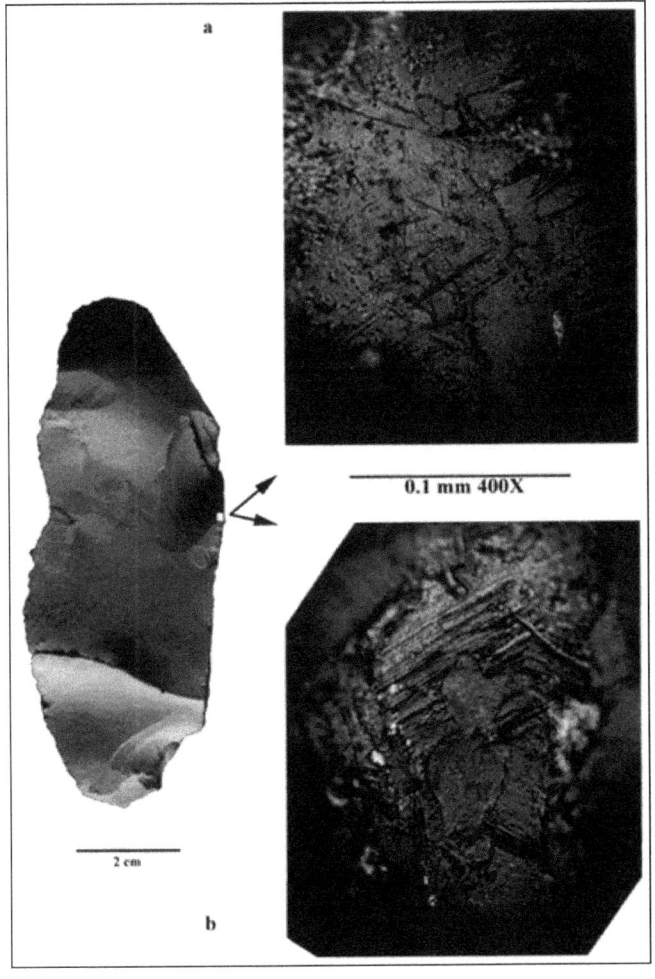

Figure 7: Denuziller casting image 2.

Another advantage of Nomarski optics is that image resolution increases and depth of field decreases as magnification increases (Kay 1998:746). Such an increase in resolution is not possible with incident-light microscopes, but is similar to scanning electron microscopes. As Kay (1998:746) points out, these resolution characteristics are ideal for viewing the polish characteristics and striations associated with a feature thereby allowing for detailed inferences of tool use and worked material to be made.

Kay (1998:746) states that the use of Nomarski optics has received limited attention in the field of use-wear analysis. This lack of attention may be changing, though. Petraglia et al. (1996:129) mention the use of Nomarski optics, albeit at lower magnifications. Also, attempts were made to obtain a reflected-light microscope with Nomarski optics at the University of Iowa. The Texas Archeological Research Laboratory at the University of Texas (Austin) recently converted an incident-light microscope so that it could also use reflected light and equipped it with Nomarski optics (Dale Hudler 2003, personal communication) and is beginning to incorporate use-wear analyses using Nomarski optics into its research program.

Examination of Casts and Experimental Tools

The artifact cast is first removed from the plastic curation bag in which it is stored, paying close attention to not touch any surface of the cast that will be scanned for wear features. This is necessary since oils from the skin can obscure wear features on the cast's surface. All casts have a thick portion below the portion representing the original artifact's surface. This thicker portion is a result of the epoxy pooling in the mold surrounded by the dental putty dam and once hardened, it provides an ideal edge or surface for handling the artifact. The next step is to anchor the cast to a metal slide mount. This is best accomplished by placing molding clay on the slide mount of sufficient size to hold or anchor the cast so that it remains immobile during examination. With the slide mount and attached molding set on a table or stable surface, the cast is manually pressed into the molding clay with one's thumbs. It is important to wear latex gloves or have a latex barrier between the cast and any skin surfaces that might come into contact with the cast during the anchoring process. The cast must be forced into the molding clay to the degree needed to prevent its own weight from causing it to shift or settle and to prevent inertia from causing any shifting while the slide mount is manipulated on the microscope stage. Once the cast is sufficiently anchored, a blast of compressed air is used to remove any objects from the cast's surface. Next the slide mount is fixed in mounts on the microscope stage and held in place by a spring-tension arm so that it can be manipulated horizontally during examination.

Scanning the artifact cast began at a magnification of 100X. The scanning process employed slightly overlapping and parallel transects to ensure that the entire cast surface had been examined. Any edge damage observed, whether associated with polishes or not, its location on the cast, and its attributes, were documented in writing. When polishes were observed, magnification was increased to 200X and 400X in order to view all of the feature's attributes and accurately describe them. All observed polishes, or in some instances areas that contained multiple polishes, were sequentially labeled numerically or alphabetically. Polishes only described in writing were given a numerical designation, and those documented both in writing and with a photomicrograph were given an alphabetic label. For example, area 3 would represent the third observed polish documented only in writing, and area B would be the second polish of which a photomicrograph had been taken.

A microscope mounted 4 x 5 camera back and Polaroid P55 positive/negative film were used to take photomicrographs of features that were either unique or representative of the wear observed on a tool or specific portion of a tool. The Polaroid film produced a 4 x 5 print and a 4 x 5 negative of each photo-documented feature. The photo axis was marked on each photomicrograph along with the artifact's provenience identification and a brief description of the wear feature. Each negative was placed in a plastic archival negative sleeve and stored with its associated photomicrograph in a transparent photo archival sleeve. The location of the feature was then marked on the artifact drawing or photograph.

All of the archaeological artifacts had been drawn in France when the silicon molds were produced. Locations of observed wear features were marked on these drawings by making a pinprick through them and labeling the feature on the reverse side. The artifact or cast on the slide mount was then oriented with the drawing and the photo axis of a particular photomicrograph or series of photomicrographs was drawn across the artifact with a straight edge. Such notation allows the photomicrographs to be correctly oriented to the tool during interpretation and such orientation is necessary when assessing tool movement and polish development. In most cases, multiple photo axes were used during the examination of a single artifact, and these were a result of the artifact or cast being re-oriented on the slide mount multiple times in order to better view wear features.

In some instances, a full examination of the cast revealed no wear features. When this occurred, the cast was re-oriented on the slide mount in such a way as to change its planar orientation with respect to the optics. As was noted above (Figure 6), slight changes in planar orientation can dramatically affect the visual expression of a feature's attributes. The same is true when considering the larger artifact surface. If no features are observed during an initial examination, one cannot assume that the tool (or cast) is devoid of them. The planar orientation of the artifact and/or the polarization plane of the light may be such that features are not visible to an observer. During the analysis of the Solutré specimens, artifacts were re-oriented on the slide mount and re-analyzed if the initial exam revealed no evidence of use. Only after a second evaluation with negative results was a tool classified as having no observed wear.

Once an artifact or cast had been thoroughly examined and all wear features documented, a specific file was created for the artifact. This file contained all of the pertinent information for the artifact: 1) a drawing or photograph of the artifact or cast on which are marked the photo axes for each photomicrograph and the locations of all documented wear features, 2) a note sheet containing the written descriptions of the wear features and associated edge damage recorded during observation, and 3) a photo sleeve containing all of the photomicrographs and associated negatives. The data contained in these artifact folders were interpreted and entered into a database used to analyze the recorded wear features and technological patterns. These data and analytical results are discussed in Chapters 6 and 7.

CHAPTER 4: EXPERIMENTAL REPLICATION

BACKGROUND

Experimentation has long been an important aspect of use-wear studies and began in the late 19th century (Sehested 1884; Spurrel 1884). Early experimentation programs, much like modern ones, attempted to reproduce the macroscopic wear patterns observed on archaeological specimens, but these early endeavors did not always employ systematic or replicable methodologies. This made comparisons of results obtained by separate researchers difficult if not impossible. Curwen (1930) incorporated two innovative aspects, which are commonplace in modern experimentation programs: photography and documentation of the length of time that a tool was used. Photography allows researchers to visually justify their interpretations and also allows for the incorporation of the work of others into an analysis. The use of photography has created a large database of wear features in the published literature that is available to all. The time that an experimental tool is used has long been recognized as an important variable to record (Crabtree and Davis 1968; Kantman 1971; Sonnenfeld 1962). Keller (1966) advocated the measurement of the number of strokes rather than simply the time used.

Early in its use, experimentation was used to demonstrate that the wear observed on prehistoric tools was not always cultural in origin (Moir 1914; Warren 1914). This had important implications. Archaeologists must demonstrate that wear patterns are not natural in origin before they can be used to make inferences about prehistoric human behavior. There are numerous experimental studies that have focused solely on natural processes and the wear traces they can leave behind (e.g., Levi-Sala 1986).

Semenov (1964) is well known for his use of experimentation. His interpretations of archaeological materials were well-supported since they were based on an experimentation program that controlled for a large number of variables. Experimentation programs undertaken by Keller (1966), Ranere (1975), and Tringham et al. (1974) were similar in that they attempted to control for a wide range of factors so that more accurate interpretations of prehistoric tool use could be made.

Any use-wear analysis, whether it utilizes low or high-power methodologies, is reliant on an experimental program and database. The most direct way to understand what sorts of edge damage, striations, and polishes result from specific motions and specific types of worked material is with controlled experimentation. A controlled program provides analogs that allow a researcher to infer tool use and worked material when analyzing an archaeological collection.

Binford (1983:36) describes the need to develop a body of theory that describes the relationships between statics and dynamics and terms this middle-range theory. With reference to use-wear analysis, the statics are the tools that have been recovered from the contemporary archaeological record and the wear features that exist on their surfaces. The dynamics are the past human actions and worked materials that created these features and that obviously cannot be directly observed by the archaeologist. Middle range research (Binford 1983:49) is the expression of middle-range theory that allows one to give meaning to the use-wear record. Middle range research is crucial in archaeology and critical in use-wear studies. Experimental programs using replicated stone tools are the most common form of research associated with use-wear analysis and the development of the associated middle-range theory. We must have an experimentally generated baseline of wear features, the motion of tool use, the worked material, and the span of time that created them if we are to interpret and attribute meaning to wear features observed on prehistoric artifacts and infer the use and function of lithic tools. Use-wear experimentation, thus, is a tool of middle range research that leads to the evaluation of general theories concerning stone tool technology and its relation to human adaptation and culture change as they relate to lithic technology.

Experimentation typically involves making replicas of the tool types recovered at a site and using them in ways and on the types of materials that a researcher considers relevant to reconstructions of prehistoric behavior. These considerations of relevancy are based on the material record recovered from the site. These replicated stone tools are then examined and used as a comparative database to examine and interpret an archaeological assemblage.

There are a variety of approaches to experimentation. Some researchers perform their experiments under laboratory conditions, meaning that they wear gloves and the experiments may be performed under strictly controlled conditions. It is difficult to assume that such experiments can be used to accurately infer patterns of prehistoric tool use, since such tool use occurred under conditions nowhere near those of a laboratory. Therefore, many experimentation programs conduct the tool use in field conditions.

One limitation with experimentation is that making one to one correlations assumes that all the variables surrounding the formation of edge damage and polishes can be or are known (Cook and Dumont 1987:55). While this assumption may not always be warranted, experimentation is the only avenue we have for evaluating wear traces observed on archaeological specimens. Cook and Dumont (1987:53) point out that experimental data should not become an end to themselves and should be applied in the interpretation of wear traces with caution. This can be a defeating and limiting perspective. It is necessary for use-wear analysts to develop an experimental framework, with well-documented comparative controls, to be used for analysis and comparison. This framework can be effective for attempting to determine prehistoric tool use, even if we cannot control for every possible prehistoric variable. One important consideration with experimentation is that the results of an experiment, or set of experiments, can be independently tested and confirmed by other researchers. If the variables of an experimental program are omitted, the experiment becomes unrepeatable and nonscientific (Odell 1975:227).

RECORDED USE-WEAR ATTRIBUTES

The Solutré experimental program is discussed in detail below, but it is necessary to describe the types of wear features and their respective attributes that were recorded on the experimental replicas and used to interpret the archaeological use-wear features during microscopic examination.

The examination of experimental tools combines the identification and interpretation of microscopic edge damage, microscopic traceological attributes (after Semenov 1964), and "polish" attributes (see Keeley 1974, 1980; Newcomer and Keeley 1979; Hurcombe 1988:4) in an attempt to infer tool use. Recording a variety of use-wear attributes on experimental tools allows for more detailed determinations of worked material and mechanics of tool use to be made with reference to the archaeological sample. Numerous studies have identified the need to record a variety of attributes so that detailed and accurate determinations of tool use and worked material are possible (see Kay 1996, 1998; Shea 1987; Vaughan 1985). The attributes recorded in the analysis of the experimental and archaeological use-wear samples are: 1) the type and degree of additive and/or abrasive polish development; 2) the absence/presence of striations, striation density and orientation relative to the tool edge; 3) the presence of abrasive particles trapped in polish; 4) the presence and location of crystallization associated with a polish; 5) location of the polish (e.g. tool edge, interior location of tool surface); and 6) presence/absence, extent, and characteristics of edge damage.

Abrasive or Attritional Polish

Abrasive wear features can be divided into three principal categories (see Kay 1998:756): 1) Extensive developed polish (EDP), 2) Intermediate developed polish (IDP), and 3) weak developed polish (WDP). As a whole, these features are produced by abrasion or attrition of the artifact's surface during use.

Abrasive EDPs exhibit a smooth surface texture (flat and relatively featureless), are highly reflective, and are broad in area. There is some variability in their expression, and additional EDP characteristics can include: 1) striae that lack depth or definitive cross-sections, and 2) well-developed rounding of edges and arrises. These polishes are oftentimes a by-product of long-term contact with soft materials that are also associated with abrasives and have been termed abrasive planing (Kay 1998:756). Other contact materials, though, can create abrasively planed features. Such examples would be long term contact and movement within a haft element (e.g. Banks 2002b; Kay 1998:757).

Abrasive IDPs result from more brief periods of contact between a tool and worked material. As a rule, their surface textures are rough and grainy, or matte in appearance, because the contact period was not sufficient to produce a highly reflective polish. Kay (1998:756) reports that this form of abrasive polish typically results from working harder contact materials, and consequently they tend to exhibit a narrow zone of contact with the worked material. Abrasive WDPs are weakly developed and may exhibit faint striations. These polishes are commonly associated with extremely brief contact between a tool and the worked material, and my experiments have shown them to be a common by-product of tool prehension during use (Appendix B-1c). Abrasive WDPs tend to be small in size and are isolated or localized in nature, meaning that there are generally no other traces of use in their immediate vicinity.

The features classified as abrasive do not all have a similar origin. Many features classified as abrasive were caused by attrition of the tool's surface from their origin until the formation of wear ceased. However, it is apparent that some abrasive features were originally microplating (see below) events. In these instances, after an additive feature's formation ceased (described below), continued use of the tool served to abrade the additive polish's surface. This formational history can be identified when remnants of microplating are still visible in what outwardly appears to be an abrasive wear feature. These remnants are typically present on the borders or edges of these features with a composite history of formation.

Additive Polish

Additive polishes can also be categorized as EDPs, IDPs, or WDPs as well, but their formation is in sharp contrast to abrasive wear. Additive polishes represent the build-up of soluble inorganic residues that form and bond to the tool surface that was in contact with a worked material. The material that goes into solution during tool use, or becomes a soluble gel, is in all likelihood principally composed of silica (Kay 1996:658–660, 1998:756–758; see also Mansur 1982; Vaughan 1985). The term used to define such additive polishes is "microplating" (Kay 1998:745, 2000:178; Kay and Solecki 2000:33). These residues are inorganic because they cannot be removed with acids or bases, and the inability to remove them with ultrasonic methods demonstrates that they are permanently bonded to the tool's surface. Microplating can consist of a single layer of the residue and is typified by a grainy or matte surface texture. These polishes can also be composed of multiple microplating events, another common characteristic of additive wear. Multiple layers of microplating allow one to follow the sequence of tool use, and such features can provide the potential to identify changes in use and worked material for a single tool. When multiple layers of microplating are present, they will fill in previously striated polishes, leaving only faint remnants of the prior striae. Another common feature of microplating is the desiccation crack. These cracks most likely form when the soluble gel hardens and bonds to the tool surface, much like the cracks that develop in mud as it dries in the sun.

Another characteristic associated with additive wear is the rounding of tool edges and arrises due to the accumulation of microplating on these surfaces. Rounding can occur due to attrition, but this is rarer. In most instances when a tool edge becomes dull, it is due to the build up of microplating around or over it. The microplating serves to smooth and round the edge such that it can no longer cut. This type of feature is commonly observed and will be discussed in detail when the features associated with specific experimental and archaeological tools are described.

A final characteristic of microplating is the presence of crystallization. The origin of this attribute is not clearly understood, but it most likely is related to the formation and/or hardening of the soluble gel. This attribute and its characteristics are described in greater detail below.

As mentioned above, it is not uncommon to see attributes consistent with both abrasive and additive wear formation in a single feature. Some features may have been initially abrasive and then covered by microplating during prolonged tool use. An opposite scenario has also been observed in which remnants on the edge of the feature are indicative of microplating, but prolonged use and the presence of abrasive served to abrade much of the microplating event's surface.

Striations

Striations, or use-generated scratches, are important attributes relating to tool edge orientation during use and the sequence of use if multiple use episodes are represented. The presence and character of striations can also provide additional support for the general class of worked material when other wear attributes are taken into consideration. Striations typically occur on the leading edge of the tool surface. Hard materials tend to produce narrow polish zones with densely packed striations. These striations range from fine, faint striae to striae that have recognizable cross-sections. Softer materials may also produce polished areas that contain striations. These striations are typical with prolonged use and may be produced by grit adhering to the worked material. Striations are common with microplating events, or additive polishes. In these situations, striations are crucial for identifying differences in tool orientation during the layering of the microplating, and thereby indicating potential differences in function. For example, a projectile point may have been used as a projectile, a cutting implement, and again as a projectile. It is the striae present in the additive polish events that allow the researcher to identify these changes in tool function for a single tool. Multi-directional striations can also indicate the reorientation of a tool during a single use episode.

Moderately abrasive features may also exhibit striations, although these tend to be fine and shallow since they have been etched into the stone surface, which is more durable than the surface of microplating.

Abrasive Particles

Striated additive polishes often contain the particles responsible for creating the striations. Abrasive particles can become trapped in these polishes during their formation and when associated with striations will be located towards the distal portion of a striation, thus indicating the direction of tool motion during that specific microplating event. The source of abrasive particles can be either the worked material or the tool itself. Kay and Solecki (2000) have documented particles of antler incorporated into additive features on experimental burins. Abrasives are not uncommon with harder and more brittle worked materials, such as bone or antler. Abrasive particles can also be present during the working of soft materials such as meat and hide since these materials are not devoid of dirt or grit during their manipulation with a stone tool, although they are less frequent than what is observed with harder worked materials.

Crystallization

Crystallization filaments commonly occur with additive polishes or the formation of microplating events. The generation of crystallization filaments seems to be a by-product of the formation of soluble inorganic residue or microplating. These crystallized portions of the microplating appear as very bright white filaments fixed to the edge of a polish. The examination of experimental tools indicates that crystallization occurs at and beyond the polish border, on its trailing side, thereby indicating tool motion during use (Kay 1998:757). It also is not uncommon to see crystallization filament fragments trapped in the body of an additive polish and, for the purposes of this analysis, these are referred to as 'spot crystallization'. It is likely that these are the visible remnants of large crystallization filaments that have been fragmented and incorporated into microplating events. With experimental tools, spot crystallization is common on tools that were used in repetitive back and forth motions. Such a pattern is not surprising since crystallization filaments always form on a polish's trailing edge, and back and forth motion would effectively fragment crystallization filaments and incorporate them into the body of a microplating event.

Polish Extent and Location

The locations of polishes, whether they are abrasive or additive in nature, allow for inferences of the hardness of worked material, and whether or not a tool was hand-held or hafted. Soft contact materials will yield to a tool's working edge thereby producing an invasive zone of contact between the material and the tool edge. Therefore, work on a soft contact material such as hide or an animal carcass during butchery can produce wear features not only on the tool edge but also well into the body of the tool. In contrast to this, hard materials do not yield to a tool's working edge, thereby producing a relatively narrow zone of tool to material contact. Wear features produced by hard materials can also exhibit a beveled zone of wear (Appendix B-5c).

There are exceptions to the cases described above. For example, a burin or blade used to work an existing groove in antler will produce invasive wear traces. However, these invasive wear traces will have attributes associated with work on hard contact materials. Therefore, polish location by itself cannot be used alone to determine the type of worked material, but acts as one of the many variables that must be considered when making a determination of tool use and worked material.

Edge Damage

As has been discussed earlier, any use-wear analysis should incorporate attributes viewed at high magnifications with those viewed at lower magnifications. Even studies that use higher magnifications and that are more focused on polishes need to incorporate other attributes such as edge damage into their interpretations. The majority of edge damage descriptions and classifications have been done with lower magnification stereomicroscopes. While areas of polish development and striations are sometimes visible with stereomicroscopes, the most visible and more easily interpreted type of wear visible with such equipment is edge damage. The characteristics and placement of edge damage can provide clues to manner in which a prehistoric tool was used. Odell (1975:232) defines the important elements or attributes of edge damage as: 1) the shape of the scar, 2) the size of the scar, 3) the definition of the scar along its rear border, and 4) the distribution of scarring along a utilized edge. Prost's (1993) work provides a standardized description of the types of edge damage targeted with a low-power approach. It is important in a low-power approach that the analysis of edge damage be integrated with an analysis of the form of the tool, edge angles, and any other relevant attributes of tool morphology (Odell 1975:230; Tringham 1971). An excellent example of such an approach is the analysis of Paleoindian assemblages performed by Wilmsen (1970). The scars produced by working on "soft" materials are generally scalar shaped. Since the worked material is soft and not resistant, flake removals occur slowly and they are generally small in size. Soft materials include hide, meat, and fleshy plants. Scars that result from working on "hard" materials such as bone, or antler are initially scalar in shape, but microflake scars with step terminations usually replace these. Because the worked material is highly resistant, these scars form fairly quickly. There is also a "medium" category that includes hard and soft woods. The flake removals from working "medium" materials are scalar with a variety of shapes, such as semicircular, triangular, and trapezoidal. Working harder woods will eventually produce step scars, but on a much smaller scale than work on "hard" materials. Scalar scars produced by working woods are smaller and shallower than those produced by working "hard" materials. They also may become more abraded and have a fuzzy appearance (Tringham et al. 1974:191).

SOLUTRÉ EXPERIMENTAL PROGRAM

This study's experimental program incorporated a variety of lithic raw materials, tool types, activities, and worked materials. Butchery and subsequent animal product processing (hide scraping, bone work, etc.) are well represented, but other activities were incorporated into the sample as well. It has been pointed earlier that there are a wide range of tool types represented in a number of the assemblages recovered from Solutré which suggests that activities other than carcass butchery might have been conducted on the site both prior and subsequent to the dispatching of large game. Thus, the experimental program included the use of tool types and other worked materials that one might expect to see in a campsite rather than a kill site setting.

This experimental program by itself surely has a number of gaps with reference to tool types and worked materials. However, the analysis of the archaeological specimens and interpretation of their wear features was not conducted with these gaps left unfilled. Marvin Kay at the University of Arkansas maintains an extensive experimental database consisting of a wide range of tool types used to process a variety of worked materials. The photomicrographic documentation of wear features observed and recorded on these additional experimental tools was consulted during and after the examination of the Solutré materials.

The combination of my experiments with the experimental database at the University of Arkansas can be considered exhaustive because they collectively represent a large number and variety of tool types and a variety of activities. Also important is the fact that a number of researchers have participated in both of their formations. One factor that can improve the efficacy of an experimental database, when making comparisons to archaeological specimens, is the number of tool users represented in an experimental program. Individuals vary in strength, the manner in which they hold a tool, and the physical motions they use to perform a task, all of which affect the formation of wear features and the expression of their attributes. Such a structure introduces user-specific variability since two experimenters using the same tool type to perform the same activity might produce wear features that exhibit some variability in their expression. One must assume that the tools that compose an archaeological assemblage were used by a variety of users and that prehistoric use-wear features might exhibit some variability even if the task was identical. If the experimental program has also incorporated user variability, one can assume that archaeological tool use inferences derived from the experimental database will be more accurate.

For example, an analysis of two archaeological specimens of the same tool type and recovered from the same archaeological context may exhibit features that, on a gross scale, appear to be different or unrelated with reference to worked material. Thus, the analyst might assign different uses to these tools, or be unable to explain this variability. However, if the experimental database used to interpret these wear patterns has been created by multiple users, the analyst might be able to see a wide range of variability in how features related to a specific activity and worked material are expressed. Therefore, the features observed on the archaeological specimens may fall within this range of variability, and the analyst can assign the same use and worked material to them and justify such a designation.

The experimental program associated with the analysis of the Solutré materials utilized a variety of high-quality cherts and flints. The majority of the tools were made from Edwards chert from central Texas. Other lithic materials included flints obtained from geologic contexts within several kilometers of Solutré, the Swiss Alps, and the northwestern coast of France (Ault). While it is important to include the same raw material type(s) as those recovered from the site in an experimental program, if all of the experimental tools are made from high quality cryptocrystalline stone, one can assume that tool use inferences will be based on an appropriate sample of experimentally generated wear features. This is due to the fact that wear features are comparably expressed on tools, both archaeological and experimental, made from high quality tool stone (Akoshima and Frison 1996). All of these materials used in the Solutré experimental program can be described as high-quality cryptocrystalline stone, and there is no obvious variation in the expression or formation of use-wear attributes on them that is attributable to raw material type. In short, comparing the experimental wear features to the features observed on the Solutré artifacts is appropriate even though the lithic materials came from a number of different geologic contexts or sources.

Cleaning and Exhaustion of Experimental Tools

One of the key issues addressed during the Solutré analysis, and a question important to understanding technological decisions, is when was a tool considered to be exhausted and what measures, if any, were taken to prolong a tool's use life. As was discussed above, microplating can form on a tool edge and, if intermediately or extensively developed, make the edge non-functional. Prehistoric users of the tool had no knowledge of this process but certainly were aware of the decreased efficiency of the employed edge of the tool. During the examination of archaeological specimens, broad, deep, and long striations, running parallel to the edge, were often observed, and these striae were usually incorporated into the observed wear features and covered with minor microplating. This means that there is evidence of further tool use following the creation of the striations that run parallel to the edge. This feature attribute also has been observed on other archaeological specimens (Kay 1998), and it has been hypothesized that this attribute is a result of the prehistoric user's attempt to clean the tool's functional edge by running a finger, or an object, along the edge to remove any adhering macroscopic debris that had accumulated during tool use. The experimental program associated with this study attempted to replicate these features. During the experiments, when a tool became less effective during use, in some instances a finger was run along the tool's employed edge to remove any accumulated debris, thereby making the edge macroscopically appear to be clean and therefore functional. After this removal, tool use continued in the same manner as before the cleaning attempt. Tool use continued until the edge was no longer functional in performing the task at hand. This attribute will be referenced specifically during the detailed discussion of experimental results.

Use-Wear Results for Butchery and Related Processing Experiments

Because the killing and butchering of large game animals (primarily horse and reindeer) was unquestionably a primary activity at Solutré, a large percentage of the experimental tools was used to butcher white-tail deer (*Odocoileus virginianus*). These butchery activities included hide removal, meat removal, meat filleting, carcass disarticulation, and cutting and scraping hide after butchery. Figures depicting the microwear recorded on these tools are contained in Appendix B. While the vast majority of butchery experiments involved deer, one tool was used to butcher three birds (one duck and two geese).

WEB-1

This flake was used for approximately 55 minutes to remove the hide from a white-tail deer carcass. Area A, documented at 200X, is visible as a large region of microplating that extends well in from the tool edge. Some scalar microflake removals are visible at the tool edge. Fine striations are visible in the center of the microplating event, but large, broad, and deep striations predominate. At 400X, one observes well-developed microplating (EDP). The larger striations are broad and shallow, and some abrasive particles are present in small quantities. In the 400X photomicrograph of WEB-1A (Appendix B-1a), one can see doming of the microplating has begun to develop. While this is commonly seen in bone, and sometimes woodwork, it is interesting to note that it is present in hide/butchery work. There is also extensive crystallization at the borders of the microplating as well as spot crystallization. Typical of butchering activities, one can observe cross-cutting oblique striations.

WEB-5

This tool was used briefly, approximately 14 minutes, to disarticulate limb elements during the butchery of a white-tail deer, along with meat removal from the limb elements. Tool use continued after a noted dulling or lessening of efficiency, although no hand cleaning of the tool edge was recorded. As will be discussed later, however, hand cleaning of the edge most likely occurred based on the recorded wear. At 200X, one notes the invasive extent of the intermediately developed polish (IDP), in both Areas A and B (Appendix B-2). The wear is both additive and abrasive in nature. Some minimal edge damage is visible despite the use of the tool to disarticulate limb elements. There are broad striations in the microplating visible in Area A. Area B has fine, shallow striations in the area of abrasive wear, typical of contact with hard material (i.e., bone and/or cartilage). Note the presence of domed microplating in Area B, also seen in Area A on WEB-1.

Area C, recorded at 400X, is invasive and is described as an EDP. The microplating is rounded over the tool edge, and large, broad, shallow striations are located parallel and immediately adjacent to the tool edge. These striations are likely the result of an attempt to manually clean the edge of adhering macroscopic organic debris. This tool was used in the early stages of the experimental program before this type of edge manipulation was recorded and integrated into the experimental program. Despite the lack of documentation related to edge cleaning attempts, it is evident that these striations can be attributed to manual cleaning of the tool edge since they closely correspond to features known to have resulted from such user action.

Area D is very invasive and characterized by broad, shallow striations primarily oriented parallel to the employed edge. This polish is an extensively developed microplating event with minimal spot crystallization and numerous trapped abrasives. One notes the presence of broad and arcing striations that originate perpendicular to the tool edge and progress such that they are parallel to the edge at the termination of tool motion. This type of feature is common in cutting and butchery features.

WEB-15

This tool was used to cut frozen and, later, partially thawed deer hide. Area A (200X) documents a relatively large area of weakly and intermediately developed wear. There is some slight edge rounding already beginning to develop and the polish is invasive. At this magnification, one notes that there are some striations, and the IDPs are linear in nature and run parallel to the tool's cutting edge.

At 400X, there is some spot crystallization and a small number of trapped abrasives are visible. The visible edge rounding is clearly caused by slightly abraded microplating that has been deposited on the tool's edge. Under the larger areas of microplating, the early wear appears to have been abrasive in nature because a weak abrasive polish is visible.

WEB-16

This experimental tool was used to cut fat and connective tissue from the interior of frozen, and later, partially thawed deer hide (Appendix B-3c, 3d, 4a). Area A is a region of very invasive wear. This polish is so extensively developed that even at 100X microplating events, abrasive particles, and striations are visible. At 200X, well-developed striations that run parallel, oblique, and perpendicular to the edge are visible, as are many of the principal attributes associated with butchery-related additive wear. This feature is a good example of the power and utility of Nomarski illumination for documenting polish attributes because while many important details are visible and easily documented in the 100X and 200X photomicrographs, the photomicrographs taken at 400X, and the details they provide, are impressive.

In Area A @ 400X, one notes the extensively developed microplating with significant crystallization on the interior border. Some minor spot crystallization is also present. It is important to point out the linear area of crystallization that is in the body of the microplating and oriented perpendicular to the tool edge. This crystallization is associated with an earlier episode of microplating deposition that was subsequently covered by additional polish deposition. One can easily identify the multiple layers of microplating or separate depositional episodes. All of the major microplating events and areas have some slight domes. This was also described on WEB-5. So, again we see doming develop during butchery, although there was no contact with bone or cartilage during the experiment that employed WEB-16. Perhaps the fact that the worked hide was frozen, and later partially thawed, is the reason for the doming. That increase in hardness may have mimicked harder contact materials and produced similar wear attributes.

There are some trapped abrasives, fine striae at the tool edge, and at least three broad striae in the interior portion of the polish, near the edge, and oriented perpendicular to it. These larger striae are only partially visible because they are obscured by microplating deposited on top of them. These are a result of cleaning strokes along the tool edge, and this experimentally generated attribute is commonly observed on the Solutré artifact sample.

There is some visible edge rounding, but it is very slight. In fact, the edge has a planed or beveled appearance with the slight rounding of microplating over the edge occurring late in the formation of this feature.

The feature identified as Area A(web) at 400X is part of the constellation of features documented in the 100X photomicrograph, and its right-hand border is just visible on the left-hand side of that lower magnification photo. This feature also displays domed microplating, crystallization, and cross-cutting broad and fine striations. However, it depicts the polish in a more blocky manner, and the feature has a different character than the one documented by M. Kay at 400X. This difference in appearance is a product of the Nomarski optics being at different settings when these features were documented, as well as a difference in the planar orientation of the tool. The variability observed in these two photomicrographs is a good example of how differences in the Nomarski optic settings and artifact planar orientation can affect feature expression, but interpretations of such features are not affected because the suites of attributes are still comparable.

WEB-17

This scraper on blade is made from Edwards chert and was used to scrape fat and connective tissue from thawed deer hide. Area A (200X) is characterized by a moderately developed polish with a small region of short striations oriented roughly perpendicular to the working edge. At this magnification, minor crystallization and minor edge rounding are visible. There is no visible edge damage, and the edge's irregularities are a result of the steep dorsal (scraper) retouch. The polish is not invasive except on the edge's projections.

At 400X, Area A exhibits multiple microplating events just in from the scraping edge. Minor spot crystallization is present. This microplating feature has a rough or highly textured appearance.

WEB-23

This tool is a retouched flake the distal and left lateral retouched edges of which were used to scrape the interior of a deer hide that was partially frozen at the beginning of use (Appendix B-5d, 6a, 6b). When the experiment ended, the hide was completely thawed. It should be noted that the wear features described below exhibit a wide range of variability, uncharacteristic of single function tools used on only one contact material.

Area A (400X) is a large area of invasive microplating on the distal end of the tool (Appendix B-5d). The striations are multidirectional, broad, and shallow. There are trapped abrasives, but they have an atypical blocky appearance. Their shape may be related to the fact that the hide was partially frozen during its processing. The scraping edge is well-rounded.

Area B (400X) is less invasive than Area A and not as heavily striated. In fact, there is almost a complete absence of striations. The microplating is relatively featureless and rough in texture. There is only minor rounding of the edge, and crystallization is well-developed.

Area C (400X) is very similar to Area A with respect to striation characteristics and the appearance of the microplating. In addition, the trapped abrasives are also blocky or angular in nature. Unlike Area A, this feature has some minor spot crystallization.

Area D (400X) is characterized by extensively developed microplating and a well-rounded edge. The polish is invasive with extensive crystallization on its interior border.

Finally, Area E (400X) resembles wear produced by working bone or antler. There are fine, shallow, and densely packed striations. However, the attributes more typical of wear produced by working a yielding contact material are present. The edge is well-rounded, the polish is relatively invasive, and the microplating at the edge has a rough texture typical of hide work.

WEB-24

This tool is a complete blade made from Edwards chert that was used to cut meat and connective tissue from the interior of a deer hide. When viewed from its ventral surface, the right proximal edge is the employed unit.

Area A (400X) is an area of small but roughly contiguous patches of domed microplating. This feature, and others on this tool, illustrates that working soft animal materials can produce domed additive wear. These small microplating events are invasive, which can be seen in the photomicrograph of Areas C1 and C2 at 100X. This feature is located in the same area of the employed unit as areas C1 and C2 and is identical to them with respect to its attributes.

Area B (400X) is similar to Areas A, C1, and C2, but the additive wear is larger in extent and more continuous along the edge. The microplating is domed and not striated. The central area of microplating is rounded over the edge, and the polish is invasive.

Areas C1 and C2, when viewed at 100X, are relatively non-descript. The tool edge is pristine or undamaged, while small areas of polish are present both on and in from the edge. It is apparent at lower magnifications that the cutting of tissue from the hide has left little evidence of tool use. This supports that argument that high-power examinations are needed to identify traces of use on tools that exhibit no macroscopic and even microscopic edge damage (see Symens 1986). With Nomarski illumination, small isolated areas of microplating are readily identified.

Area C1 (400X) has a rough and domed appearance, is not striated, and wraps over the tool edge. Some minor spot crystallization is present. Area C2 (400X) is located in from the edge and is characterized by two small patches of microplating and associated crystallization. There is little to no evidence of tool motion or directionality on the features documented on this tool's surface.

WEB-25

This is a double endscraper on a blade used to scrape fresh deer hide for a brief period of time (5–10 minutes). Area A (400X) is a region of abraded microplating that is well-rounded over the scraping edge (Appendix B-6c). The trapped abrasives indicate that this feature is a highly abraded microplating event. Area E (400X) is an isolated spot of microplating restricted to and rounded over a projection on the scraping edge on the same scraping edge as Area A.

Area B (400X), on the opposite scraping edge is an invasive region of abrasive wear that has a greasy luster. The edge appears to be slightly rounded. Area C, located adjacent to Area B, is also a region of invasive wear that is weakly developed. There are some faint striations at the scraping edge indicating a motion perpendicular to the edge.

WEB-44

This small blade was used to field dress a deer. The activity consisted of making the belly cut and cutting the connective tissue to facilitate gutting the animal. Little wear was observed on the tool during examination by two different researchers. Area A (400X) is wear produced by prehension. This feature is a small region of weakly developed striated microplating with multidirectional striations.

Area B (400X) is dominated by what at first appears to be microplating. Trapped particles are present in this feature. However, upon closer examination, a number of attributes not typical of additive wear are visible. The desiccation cracks are atypical of those seen on the surface of microplating, and the texture of this feature is varied. Some areas are smooth and reflective, while other areas are more textured. This feature is most likely composed of dried blood. The muted striations are probably associated with a striated wear feature on the tool's surface that has been covered with a veneer of blood.

WEB-46

This blade is made from flint from Ault, France, and was used to butcher two ducks and one Canadian goose. The butchery focused on the removal of breast meat. The distal left corner, the distal blade termination, and right lateral edge were the employed tool units.

Area B (200X) is located on the distal end of the blade. This wear feature is characterized by weakly developed wear. The curvature of this blade is so pronounced that it makes it impossible to document this feature at higher magnification. At 200 diameters it is difficult to determine if this feature is additive or abrasive. Striations are oblique to the edge and some areas of crystallization are visible. There is some minor edge damage, so the observed cutting wear was likely produced by contact with bone and cartilage.

Because the curvature of the blade was so pronounced, a cast was made of the distal portion of this tool. Area C (400X) was recorded on the cast and is characterized by a narrow zone of rough or textured wear (Appendix B-10b). There is some minor edge damage that has been rounded over by the microplating. This feature is dominated by extensive crystallization on the interior border and lesser amounts off the tool's working edge.

Butchery Wear Summary

Butchery wear is dominated by additive wear or microplating events. However, a minor amount of butchery wear can be abrasive in nature and can range from weakly developed abrasive wear to well-developed abrasive planing. Kay (1996:326) illustrates an example of abrasive planing on a flake butchery tool. For the most part, though, microplating events make up the majority of features recorded on the experimental butchery tools. These additive events are commonly associated with deep and, generally, broad striations, although fine and shallow striations are also present. These striations can be parallel, oblique, and perpendicular to the working edge, and oftentimes a combination of orientations is present. Edge damage is typically minimal, and with well-developed features, the microplating is rounded over the edge and obscures or mutes any visible edge damage. Doming of the microplating is sometimes present. The presence of this attribute is curious since it is typically associated with work on harder contact materials. The presence of doming is most likely a result of contact with tendons, cartilage, and bone during carcass disarticulation. The last attribute of wear associated with butchery events is that they are invasive, meaning that they are observed at the edge and also well in from the edge in an interior portion of the ventral and dorsal surfaces. Invasive location is a result of the yielding nature of soft contact materials (flesh and hide) and the fact that worked material wraps around the working edge of the tool. This attribute is in sharp contrast to the wear observed on tools used to work more resistant contact materials. Crystallization is also common on butchery features. Crystallization filaments are commonly observed on the interior border of microplating events, and spot crystallization is ubiquitous.

In addition to butchery, it was necessary to conduct other experiments using a range of tool types, a range of motions, and a variety of worked materials. When structuring an experimental program, it is important to hypothesize about what activities and worked materials might have been present during the prehistoric use of the archaeological sample. It cannot be assumed that these hypotheses take into account all of the activities and worked materials that comprised the prehistoric uses associated with an archaeological assemblage. One should also include an inductive approach to an experimental program. Many of the experiments carried out during this study did just that. An aspect of some of the assemblages recovered from Solutré is that they contain a wide range of tools not typically associated with kill/butchery sites but rather more common in campsite or special activity site assemblages. Therefore, some experiments included the manipulation or processing of bone, antler, wood, and soft plant materials. These experiments also incorporated a variety of tool types and tool motions.

Woodworking

A number of experiments focused on processing both hard and soft wood, and these wood samples ranged from green to dry. Actions consisted of whittling or bark removal, sawing, planing, and scraping. Many tools had edges that were used for multiple functions based on the assumption that prehistoric tool edges were not restricted to a single function. The end products of these experiments were projectile shafts and wood handles.

WEB-13

This blade was used to cut and plane green hard wood. The majority of use involved a planing motion aimed at removing bark from the branch. Area A1 (400X) is an area of intermediately developed microplating (Appendix B-3a). There are abrasive particles incorporated into the polish, but they are not associated with any striations. The polish is matte in appearance and not reflective. Crystallization on the polish's borders is present, albeit minor, and spot crystallization is readily visible. In Area A2 (400X), the same matte and relatively featureless microplating events are visible. Some abrasive particles are incorporated into the microplating, but are not as predominant as in Area A1. There are some broad striations, but they have been filled in such that they are not predominate attributes. Bi-directional crystallization is present on the polish borders, along with spot crystallization.

WEB-18

This flake was used to scrape and plane dry hard wood. Area B (400X) shows an invasive area of moderately developed microplating that has just begun to cover the higher portions of the surface's microtopography (Appendix B-1d). This microplating extends into the body of the tool before thinning. The edge is rounded by microplating and some minor spot crystallization is visible at the edge. There are numerous trapped abrasives. One commonly observed abrasive is a relatively large particle that has a rounded and dark appearance. These particles are possibly phytoliths incorporated into microplating events.

WEB-41

This hand-held experimental tool is a flake made from Edwards Plateau chert that was used to cut and saw a green maple branch. Smaller twigs were removed by sawing with the serrated edge. The same edge was used to plane and scrape away bark and underlying wood tissue. The edge opposite the serrated edge was used for limited cutting and planing. This tool was used until the primary edge was no longer effective for cutting. An attempt was made to clean the edge with a finger, but the edge was never retouched. This heavy utilization with no rejuvenation and the cleaning strokes were an attempt to recreate patterns seen on the Solutré tools.

Areas A1 and A2 illustrate an large area of blocky and domed microplating with both broad and fine striations (Appendix B-9a). There is moderate edge damage and minor crystallization on the borders of the wear feature along with minimal spot crystallization. This feature is moderately invasive.

Area B (400X) is a small area of moderately developed invasive additive polish. Striations are oriented perpendicular to the working edge. There is an absence of crystallization. At 200X, Area C is displayed as an interiorly located abraded microplating event with broad shallow striations oriented perpendicular to the working edge. At 400X, crystallization is readily apparent and the wear is weakly developed (Appendix B-9b). Area D, at 100X, is expressed as an area of moderately developed abrasive wear in an interior location. This wear feature was produced by prehension.

WEB-45

Although this blade was not used to work wood, it is described here because the documented wear is very similar to that described on the other tools above. This blade made from Edwards chert was used to cut pumpkin rind with a sawing motion. Area A at 400X is expressed as an area of domed microplating surrounded by smaller and less well-developed spots of additive polish (Appendix B-10c). The large additive feature is noticeably domed and much like other features documented on tools used to work harder materials. It has extensive crystallization on both its exterior and interior margins. The placement of the crystallization is a result of the back and forth cutting motion. Some minor striations, oriented perpendicular to the tool edge, are visible.

Summary

Additive features that are often striated dominate the wear documented on tools used to work wood. These additive features typically have a blocky appearance and are matte in texture. This microplating can be developed enough to round over the working edge. Also, the working edges of the wood working tools usually exhibit minor to moderate edge damage.

In the additive wear, abrasive particles are common and are possibly phytoliths that have been incorporated into the microplating events. It is not uncommon for these microplating events to have a slightly domed appearance. Finally, crystallization is usually present, but it is typically minimally developed. It is uncommon to see large crystallization filaments associated with wear features generated by processing wood.

Bone work

WEB-26bis

This tool is a burin made on a small blade of Niobrara jasper from northwestern Kansas. It was used to groove the spine of a soaked bison scapula so that it could be removed. The tool was examined without being cleaned, and the lack of cleaning is clearly visible in the photo-documented wear features.

Area A is a long narrow zone of microplating along the burin facet (Appendix B-7b). There are numerous, fine, and densely packed striations, along with some minor doming in the lower corner of the photomicrograph. There is some crystallization, but the majority of the bright reflective particles are microscopic fragments of bone. Area B is an invasive region of striated microplating that is highly textured and that has a greasy luster. Numerous bone particles are visible.

WEB-27

This tool is a burin on a break made from Niobrara jasper. The burin bit was used to groove soaked bison scapula along both sides of the dorsal spine to facilitate its removal, and the tool was used only briefly. When it began to become less effective at the grooving task, the user's thumb and forefinger were used to remove macroscopic bone debris from the bit and facets. It was used briefly after this cleaning attempt and then when it was no longer effective, it was retired without being rejuvenated.

At 100X, one can see extensively developed microplating around the burin bit but cannot clearly identify any specific attributes (Appendix B-7d). With a magnification of 200X, it is clear that this feature is an extensively developed polish with multidirectional striations, numerous abrasives, and crystallization. At 400X, it is clear that there are multiple episodes of microplating deposition with associated spot crystallization and crystallization filaments. The later episodes of microplating are domed. On the interior border of the polish there are small sets of fine and densely packed striations. The cleaning attempt is evidenced by two long, broad, and deep striations at and parallel to the facet edge. The interior most striation is very broad and completely covered with microplating while the striation on the edge is still clearly visible. This feature is relatively invasive because during its use it was inserted into the groove along the scapula spine thereby allowing invasive contact between the tool and the worked material.

WEB-28

This tool is a blade made from Niobrara jasper with one retouched edge and another that is naturally backed. The retouched edge has a slightly denticulated form and was used to slot and cut an existing groove along the junction of a bison scapula blade and dorsal spine. The tool was rejuvenated once during use to re-denticulate the edge. After this retouching event, the tool was used until it was exhausted or no longer functional.

Area A, when viewed at 200X, is a large region of highly abraded microplating with strong directionality. The striations are fine and densely packed, as is seen on many of the other wear features documented on tools used to work hard materials. The polish is invasive due to the tool edge's placement in a pre-existing groove in the scapula. At 400X, the fact that this feature is abraded microplating is evident. Trapped abrasives are present in the abraded polish. Some well-developed spot crystallization is visible in the center of the photomicrograph. In both photomicrographs there is a blurry sheen over the feature. This veneer is most likely bone residue since this tool was examined without any prior cleaning.

WEB-29

This experimental tool is a blade made from Niobrara jasper with a denticulated working edge used to deepen a slot in a preexisting groove along the dorsal spine of a soaked bison scapula. Area A is a large region of polish along the denticulated edge and is highly textured, or rough in appearance, and at 200X appears to be a well-developed abrasive polish (Appendix B-8c). The worn area is restricted to the edge, and the densely packed striations are oriented parallel and oblique to the edge as a result of the sawing motion of the tool. At 200X, though, there are numerous spots in the polish that appear to be abrasive particles.

When viewed at 400X, it becomes clear that these are indeed particles trapped in the polish. They are most likely fragments of bone and microflake removals from the tool edge. The presence of trapped abrasives indicates that this polish was initially additive and then became highly abraded as tool use continued. This is also supported by the almost complete absence of crystallization. There is only one small area of crystallization on the interior border of the polish and no spot crystallization. The abrasive nature of the later wear probably removed all but a few remnants of the crystallization that is typical of microplating events. The two photomicrographs of this feature at different magnifications illustrate the necessity of documenting and observing wear features at magnifications above 200X when possible because feature attributes are more clearly observed.

WEB-30

This experimental tool is a small broken flake made from Niobrara jasper. The distal break and lateral edge form an opportunistic burin bit (burin on break) that was used to groove a dry bison scapula dorsal spine in order to facilitate its removal. The tool was hand-held and used for approximately 40 minutes, although it was largely ineffective at its task as the bone had not been soaked overnight in water. The tool was examined without being ultrasonically cleaned.

Area A was documented on the burin bit. At 200X, the bit is visibly damaged as a result of working unsoaked bone which is very hard. This damage at the tip has probably removed most of whatever wear features formed on the functional edge.

When viewed at 400X, the small bright spots of wear seen at 200X are clearly a small area of abrasive wear with an orientation parallel to the tool's long axis, typical of wear on a burin bit. The wear is minimal. It is also clear at this magnification that the large white particle is bone residue and not a bundle of crystallization filaments.

Summary

Bone wear has a wide range of expression and can be additive or abrasive in nature. These features are commonly striated with numerous, fine, and densely packed striations. Abrasive particles are usually present in striated microplating events. Due to the hardness of the contact material, bone wear is restricted to the tool's edge. The only exception is when a tool edge is placed into an existing groove or slot. This invasive placement allows bone to contact the tool surface well in from the working edge. The contact material hardness also results in many wear features at the tool edge having a planed or beveled appearance.

Additive bone wear features are commonly domed and many of those created by this experimental program have a greasy luster. Another common attribute of bone wear is the presence of well-developed crystallization. Because of the heavy crystallization, on tools used for any length of time, spot crystallization is readily visible in the microplating events. Finally, if the bone has not been soaked prior to being worked, it is so hard and resistant that the tool edge breaks down quickly and little wear remains on the employed unit.

Antler work

A number of experimental tools, from a variety of raw material types, were produced in order to process deer antler. Tool types included unretouched blades, retouched blades, and burins. All of the experiments used antler that had been submerged in water and soaked at least 10 hours. Some initial experiments attempted to groove and slot deer antler that had not been soaked. Stone tools are not effective when working unsoaked antler, even if the tool has a strong high angle working edge. The employed edges of the tools in the unsoaked antler experiments disintegrated in a matter of seconds, so a switch to only soaked antler in these experiments was made. It is highly unlikely that dry antler was worked on a consistent basis because it is simply too hard even for tools with strong tool edges. It is also unlikely that any use-wear features could be observed on such tools since the tool edge completely breaks down thereby removing portions of the tool edge that had been in contact with the worked material.

WEB-20

This blade is made from flint obtained several kilometers northeast of Solutré and was used to groove soaked antler. Area A (400X) is a feature characterized by abrasive wear (Appendix B-5b). One can observe a highly reflective polish with fine, densely packed striations. This type of wear is commonly observed on tools used to work antler and bone, or hard contact materials.

WEB-21

This endscraper is made from Edwards chert and was used to groove and scrape soaked antler. The majority of use was directed at shaping the antler surface with a back and forth scraping motion. Area A (400X) is an example of additive wear (Appendix B-5c). Striated microplating is visible on the interior edge of the feature, and the striations are densely packed but deeper than what is seen in Area A on WEB-20. Unstriated microplating has covered the initial microplating event. In the upper portion of this microplating event, the surface is slightly crenulated or undulating. This deformation is a product of the smooth microplating covering the initial striated microplating, but it lacks the thickness needed to completely obscure the striated topography of the feature that it covers. The microplating deposited last has some minimally developed domed features. One can also observe a few small, trapped abrasives. Spot crystallization is present, and there are well-developed crystallization filaments on the interior border of the polish and off the tool edge. Even though the contact material is hard, the tool edge has been slightly rounded by microplating. Typical of features produced by hard contact materials, it is narrow in width, restricted to the working edge, and has a planed, or beveled, appearance.

WEB-22

This experimental tool is an angled burin made from Maconnais flint and was used to groove and slot soaked antler. Area A (400X) is located on the burin bit. The microplating rounded over the bit is barely visible as it is covered by densely stacked crystallization filaments. Area B (400X) is located on the edge of the lateral burin facet. This feature's wear is characterized by slightly abraded and striated microplating. This wear signature is similar to the initial microplating event described for Web-21 Area A. The polish is restricted to the facet's edge but is not developed enough to have a beveled appearance. There is minimal edge damage, and crystallization filaments are visible just off the edge.

WEB-43

This double burin is made from Edwards chert and its bits were used to groove and slot soaked antler that had begun dry or loose its moisture content. Both bits deteriorated quickly even though the antler was not completely dry, so even partially dry antler destroys strong tool edges quickly. One burin facet was used to bi-directionally plane the partially dried antler and this is where the majority of wear was observed and recorded.

Both Areas A (400X) and B (400X) exhibit identical wear features (Appendix B-9d, 10a). As has been seen with other tools used to work antler, both features are dominated by highly abraded microplating characterized by fine, densely packed striations that are oriented perpendicular to the tool's working edge.

In Area A, at the top of the feature, there is a small area of unabraded microplating on top of the larger feature. The directionality of this later spot of additive wear is parallel to the tool's working edge. There are numerous bumps in this microplating event. These are abrasives that have been thoroughly incorporated into the microplating and covered by it. In Area B, one notes a set of short, broad striations in the center of the photomicrograph oriented perpendicular to the directionality of the larger wear feature like is seen with the small area of microplating in Area A discussed above. Both of these small attributes were created with an attempt to clean antler debris from the facet by running a thumb along the ventral surface of the burin facet.

Summary

Antler wear is similar to bone wear, and it is oftentimes difficult to distinguish between the two. Like bone, if antler is not thoroughly soaked in water prior to processing, it will quickly destroy a tool's working edge. This is even true of strong tool edges like high angled burin bits.

Antler wear can be both additive and abrasive in nature. Microplating events are often highly reflective and trapped abrasives are common. When striated, both additive and abrasive antler wear is marked by the presence of fine and densely packed striae. Wear along the tool edge is restricted to the edge and usually has a planed or beveled appearance. Although unexpected, some microplating events may be highly reflective and smooth. In these situations, it is not unusual to see domed attributes on the feature. It is common to observe heavy crystallization and associated spot crystallization. Finally, edge damage ranges from non-existent to extensive and appears to be related to the water content of the antler and the length of tool use.

Organic Remains

If not cleaned, experimental tools often display microscopic organic remains. Experimental tool WEB-44 was used to gut a deer and an additive, caked material can be observed on top of microplating events. This material had the appearance of dried or sun-baked clay, and is most likely blood adhering to the surface of the tool. Experimental WEB-46 displayed microscopic feather remains when observed prior to any cleaning. Many of the experimental tools used to work bone were examined without the standard ultrasonic cleaning. Many of the wear features documented on these tools exhibit large, white, and granular particles atop the wear features. Kay and Solecki (2000) document the presence of microscopic fragments of antler on an experimental burin. These examples suggest that archeological tools should be examined for traces of use and possible organic remains on their surfaces before they are cleaned. The presence of fragments of the worked material on the surface of a tool can be used to precisely define a worked material or materials.

However, all of these examples demonstrate the presence of organic remains on experimental tools a short time after their period of use, and one could argue that the chances of such materials remaining on a tool after being contained in a site's sediments for tens of thousands of year would be slim at best. The results of the research by Hardy et al. (2001) contradict such an argument. Their study focused on the stone tools from Starosele and Buran Kaya III, two sites in the Crimea. In this study, a sample of tools was subjected to analysis at high magnifications prior to any cleaning. Numerous examples of feather barbules, hair strands, fragments of plants, and starch grains were observed and documented. These results are remarkable considering that the tools range in age from 80,000 B.P. to 28,000 B.P. (Hardy et al. 2001:10972). The tools were then subjected to a high-power use-wear analysis at a separate lab with the researcher unaware of the results of the organic remains analysis. The use-wear analysis documented numerous features. When the use-wear results were compared with the residue analysis, in many cases use-wear features and organic residues were recorded in identical locations on the tool. There were no instances of contradictory evidence between the two independent analyses, but rather the results were either in complete agreement or could be placed in the consistent category (Hardy et al. 2001:10973–10974).

This research has broad implications because oftentimes it is difficult to precisely define a worked material. For example, wear resulting from wood working has a range of expression, and the observed attributes will vary based on the type of wood and its moisture content, sometimes making it difficult to determine if the wood was a dry soft wood or a wet hard wood. The same applies to butchery wear. Butchery wear on large game animals and avian fauna can look similar, and while the researcher can deduce that the tool was used to butcher an animal, the type of animal remains in question. The integration of high-power residue and high-power use-wear analyses has the potential to eliminate this lack of specificity.

Prehension and Hafting Wear Traces

One issue critical to studies of toolkit structure and understanding of technological organization (i.e., curated versus expedient tools) is the ability to determine whether or not a tool was hand-held or hafted. Because there are numerous published studies that document the nature and range of variation of use-wear produced by hafting (Kay 1996, 1998, 2000), all of the tools in my experiments were hand-held in an effort to augment the prehension wear feature component of the University of Arkansas' experimental database.

Hafting wear has a wide range of expression and a number of attributes may be observed in a variety of combinations (Banks 2002b; Kay 1996, 1998, 2000). First, haft wear, like other types of wear, can occur in either abrasive or additive forms. Also, the longer the period of wear generation, the greater the chance that the most visible and recognizable attributes will be abrasive in nature and prolonged use while hafted can produce extensive areas of abrasive planing on a tool (Banks 2002b). Haft wear commonly occurs over large areas, although small isolated but similar areas of polish can be present in a specific region of the tool. Another common characteristic is the presence of groups of cross cutting striations that are typically oriented oblique and/or perpendicular to one another. These striations exhibit a wide range of variation and may be fine and densely packed, narrow and deep, or broad and shallow, and a single haft feature may exhibit this entire range of variation. The variability in striation morphology is most likely a reflection of the types of material used to make the haft (e.g., wood, bone, antler). Nonetheless, it is oftentimes difficult to establish the type of material from which a haft was made. The integration of a high-power residue analysis has the potential to eliminate this lack of precision in some instances. Hardy et al. (2001) were able to determine the class of material used to haft archaeological tools based on the presence of organic residues still adhering to them. This is especially useful with tools that were used extensively while hafted and the associated haft wear is expressed as abrasive planing.

Hafting can be inferred when multiple features with these characteristics are seen in a specific region of a tool. Such features typically occur on proximal portions of tool, or areas of the tool proximal to the employed tool edge, or portions of the tool that have been retouched in such a way to facilitate placement in a hafting element (e.g., thinning of a tool blank's bulb of percussion, backing of an edge, retouch to form a shoulder).

As was indicated above, one focus of this experimental program was to attempt to create use-wear features resulting from prehension, and representative examples are described below.

WEB-11

This tool is a small blade that was used to fillet white-tailed deer meat. Area A documents a small area of moderately abraded microplating on an area of the tool's ventral surface that was in contact with the user's hand rather than the worked material (Appendix B-1c). This feature exhibits both broad and fine striations. In association with the broad striations, one can observe the abrasive particles that created them as they are incorporated into the microplating. The fine striations are shallow and densely packed. This portion of the tool did not come into contact with the meat being filleted. The abrasive particles are probably dirt or grit that was on the user's hand during use. It is important to note that contact between skin and the tool surface, during a light duty activity, was able to create a small microplating feature. Area 3 on this tool was not photodocumented but is described as weakly developed polish that occurs on high spots and ridges of the surface microtopography. There is a low frequency of trapped abrasives and small striations oriented perpendicular to the tool's long axis.

WEB-41

This experimental tool is a flake used to cut, saw, plane, and scrape a green maple branch. Area D documents a broad area of weakly developed abrasive wear with strong directionality that corresponds to the motion of tool use during the processing activity (Appendix B-9c). The broadness of this feature and its abrasive wear signature are common attributes of prehension wear.

CHAPTER 5: CURATION AND TYPOLOGY

At a coarse scale, this study is a microwear analysis of tools from the recent excavations of the cultural components at Solutré. This study describes the patterns of tool use and tool function within each cultural component and compares the results from a temporal perspective. Before there is a discussion of these results, however, an outline of the theory that serves as a backdrop for this study is warranted.

CURATION

The term "curation" and the concepts behind it are often cited in studies of hunter-gatherer technology and interpretations of the structure and variability of lithic toolkits. This term was first introduced by Binford (1973:242–244) when he defined the curated components of a toolkit to be those that were transported from place to place for multiple uses over a span of time, maintained for predicted future use, and represented an efficient reduction and use of tool stone. In subsequent publications, Binford (1977, 1979) refined the term and added to it the behaviors of recycling exhausted tools into different forms for different tasks than those that were performed with the initial tool form, as well as the concept that individual curated tools were designed to perform a variety of tasks.

Since that time, numerous others have weighed in on the topic and described the anticipated characteristics of curated technologies. Bleed (1986) focused on hunting weapons and how such components of a hunter-gatherer toolkit are designed to be either reliable or maintainable. Reliable systems tend to be used for highly specialized and repetitive activities that are predictable and such tools are designed so that their ability to function is assured (Bleed 1986:739, 741). Groups that practice an intercept strategy of hunting commonly use weapons that are designed for reliability (Bleed 1986:741). Bleed (1986:741) stated that the disadvantages of reliable weaponry are justified in situations where hunters know when and where game resources will be available and sufficient downtime will be available. An example of such a situation would be the hunting of migratory game animals at a known time and location. Such groups could have practiced either a collecting or foraging subsistence strategy. Maintainable systems are best suited for activities that are expected to be continuous but occur on a schedule that is unpredictable. This would be typical of groups that were highly mobile [foragers as defined by Binford (1980)] and unsure of when and where they would need their hunting equipment, but who had to anticipate needing that equipment at locations on the landscape where tool stone would not be available to make replacements for failed tools. Maintainable tools are also designed so that they can be easily repaired when broken, or easily modified if they are not appropriate for the task (Bleed 1986:739).

While Bleed's (1986) study focused on hunting weaponry, Bousman (1993:69) points out that Bleed's expectations apply to all tools in a toolkit. If this conclusion is correct, and I think it is, one would expect other elements of the toolkit to display traits of curation when such a technology was employed. Therefore, since human groups intercepted horse and reindeer herds at Solutré as the animals migrated between their upland and river valley grazing territories, one would expect the majority of tools in their toolkits to be marked by the characteristics associated with curation and to have been designed for reliability rather than maintainability.

Shott (1989:24) addressed the concept of curation and described the term as representing the realized utility of a tool, or in other terms, taking measures to maximize its use-life. Therefore, a crucial component in the concept of tool curation is the practice of taking measures to maximize the amount of time that an implement would spend in a lithic toolkit. Shott (1986:23) found that curated toolkits should be characterized by a reduction in the number of tool classes carried between residences, since most curated technologies are associated with highly mobile groups. Such high mobility could either be logistical or residential in nature. He stated that curated tools could be expected to be smaller and lighter and, due to the expected reduction in the number of tools in the toolkit, be used to perform a range of functions, thus becoming less specialized and more multi-functional in nature (Shott 1986:20). This matches the expectations proposed by Binford (1977, 1979) and later by Kelly (1988). Therefore, a curated tool is one that is designed to be more flexible than an expedient (sensu Binford 1979) or instant (sensu Gould 1980:72) tool. This decrease in diversity and increase in flexibility should be associated with an increase in the number (and variety) of tasks that a tool is used to perform. This can be recognized by an increase in the number of EUs per tool recognized with use-wear methods, and his review of Knudson's (1973) data show the hypothesis to be correct (Shott 1986).

Kuhn (1994) addressed the potential design and composition of curated tools and toolkits carried by mobile groups. The main factors considered in the development of his model are the potential utility of a tool and transport costs. He found that the best strategy for maximizing utility per unit mass is to produce a mobile toolkit composed of many small tools that are between 1.5 and 3 times their minimum usable size (Kuhn 1994:435). Therefore, one would expect a curated toolkit to consist of several small, functionally specialized tools (Kuhn 1994:435). Kuhn (1994:426, 435) stated that multifunctionality was not necessarily an important tool design criterion, and that multifunctionality was simply a product of curated items being part of a toolkit for a long period of time. While his findings related to tool size are consistent with others' work, his claim related to specialization at first seems to be counter to Shott's (1986) expectation of tool flexibility instead of narrow functionality.

I do not think this is the case, though, and find both models to be complementary. One must keep in mind that a toolkit may have started out as one that was composed of small functionally specific tools. However, the actual realized needs and uses of the toolkit may not have mirrored those that were originally anticipated, and functionally specific tools had to be used in an improvised manner in such scenarios over a long span of time. If a curated toolkit were to be abandoned or lost shortly after its creation, and recovered archaeologically, then one might be able to demonstrate that Kuhn's predictions are accurate. However, with curated toolkits, such a scenario is highly unlikely to happen, and the longer a curated tool is transported and used, the higher the likelihood that it will have to be used in numerous improvised situations to complete tasks for which it was not originally designed. While its morphology suggests it to be functionally specific, over the long-term there is a higher likelihood that use-wear features would demonstrate that it was used to perform a variety of tasks. Shott (1986) and Kuhn (1994) are proposing the same expectations, but are envisioning the curated toolkit at different points in time.

A modern example of this would be if one's car continued to overheat because of a faulty thermostat. One option would be to remove and replace the faulty thermostat with a new one. Needless to say, conditions might make it impractical to change the thermostat at the time at which it is discovered to be malfunctioning, or a new one may not be available. One option is to deliver a heavy blow to the thermostat so that the malfunctioning valve would become free and open. A heavy tool in the trunk's toolkit could serve this function, but one may not carry a hammer in the car's emergency toolkit. A functionally specific tool, such as a socket wrench, heavy screwdriver, etc., could be used to serve this purpose, and become general or multifunctional in nature. The same would hold true for a screwdriver being driven through an oil filter to remove it when a filter wrench is ineffective because the filter is over tightened. In each instance, one has a functionally specific toolkit, but over time unexpected situations and needs force specialized items in it to be flexible. This occurs when unexpected situations occur and access to the necessary tool(s), or time constraints, do not allow the necessary functionally specific tool to be made available or used.

If one could view the history of uses of the tools in a car's emergency toolkit when it was new, then Kuhn's (1994) prediction of functionally specific tools would hold true. If the histories of use for each tool in that toolkit could be viewed several years later, one would expect to see functionally specific tools used to complete tasks for which they were not originally designed. Accordingly, Shott's (1986) expectation of flexibility would hold true. Tools might be intended to be functionally specific, but their design and morphology are not so restrictive as to prevent their utility in situations for which they were not originally designed or intended.

Similar scenarios must have occurred in prehistoric situations and would be expected in instances in which there was no time to make a new tool, limited access to toolstone, or not enough raw material available to afford to make a new tool. In such instances, one would expect functionally specific tools to become flexible, therefore moving a toolkit from the specialized end of the continuum towards the flexible end.

In summary, curated toolkits are dominated by tools that can perform a variety of tasks, are easily and efficiently maintained, are made in advance of their anticipated use, are transported from place to place over the course of their use-life, and may be recycled into functionally different tools prior to their eventual discard. A lithic toolkit with such a technological organization is well-suited to the needs of logistically organized groups due to their increased efficiency over an expedient technology (Binford 1977:35). The same would also apply to groups that were highly residentially mobile in areas where tool stone was scarce or access was unpredictable.

As the previous examples indicate, Binford (1977, 1980) and Shott (1986:23) argue that the concepts of curation and expediency are aspects of technology that are heavily influenced by a group's subsistence and settlement organization. While it would be difficult to argue that these researchers did not acknowledge that other factors certainly influenced the expression of a specific lithic technology, others (e.g., Bamforth 1986; Odell 1996) have stated that tool curation cannot be explained by any single dominant factor, such as mobility. Bamforth (1986:48) and Odell (1996:54) discuss the multitude of factors that influence the human behaviors that lead to tool curation. While mobility is certainly an important determinant, they, along with Andrefsky (1991, 1994), argue that raw material availability and quality are more important influences. Bamforth (1986:39) points out that raw material conservation, which would have a curated signature on a recovered assemblage, would be more important than efficiency in a region marked by raw material scarcity. Therefore, one could recognize a group that practices residential mobility in an area where raw materials were scarce or of poor quality and find their toolkit to have a curated signature due to these restrictions. Such a pairing of curated technology and residential mobility structure goes counter to a theory of curation for which mobility is considered the prime determinant.

I argue that both mobility or settlement strategy and raw material availability are intertwined and it cannot be assumed a priori that one is more influential than the other. It might be possible to recognize a prehistoric group that moved about in a region with numerous but spatially limited sources of high quality raw material, but their mobility structure and resource acquisition scheduling, or the locations of resource extraction, may not have made raw material acquisition feasible whenever necessary. In this instance, one would expect a more curated technology due to limited access to stone because of scheduling and mobility. Hence, mobility was the prime mover since it limited access to stone. The opposite holds for either a logistically or residentially mobile group in a region where raw materials are scarce or access to them is limited. In these instances, it would be expected to find the use of curated technologies, but with raw material availability rather than mobility being the primary influence. Therefore, both mobility and availability must be considered as possible factors.

CURATION USE-WEAR SIGNATURES

As the above review of curation has shown, it is important for a researcher to specifically define what is meant by "curation" on a case by case basis. Odell (1996:51) points out that the various definitions of curation and subsequent ambiguities require that the term be precisely defined if it is to be used in a study of a lithic technology or technologies. For the purposes of this study, curation is used to describe a toolkit dominated by tools that can perform a variety of tasks, that are easily and efficiently maintained, that are made in advance of their anticipated use, transported from place to place over the course of their use-life, and may be recycled into functionally different tools prior to their eventual discard.

While these characteristics can be inferred with a traditional morphological and technological analysis, it has been stated previously that use-wear analysis is a necessary final step needed to support or refute hypotheses of toolkit structure and tool use. Use-wear analysis is an analytical tool that can complete a chaîne opératoire and in turn allow a determination to be made of where a technology falls on the continuum between expedient and curated.

That being said, the primary question is what use-wear signatures indicate curation? In other words, how can curation be recognized through use-wear features? This question has been discussed in the literature and the findings summarized below. I also propose two additional use-wear attributes that are indicative of curation.

Resharpening

Resharpening is considered to be a strong possible signature of tool curation since it indicates tool maintenance, and curated tools have a higher likelihood of being maintained relative to expedient ones (Bamforth 1986; Shott 1986). The principle problem with the resharpening signature is that tool retouch cannot always be considered indicative of maintenance. A tool edge on an expedient tool might be retouched to facilitate prehension or to change the angle of an edge so that it is better suited to perform a specific task. Odell (1996:) suggests that a resharpening index —Shott's (1986) ratio of total length:haft length—and the recordation of alternate beveling are two ways to recognize and quantify resharpening. Alternate beveling is not applicable to the Solutré assemblages, and a resharpening index does not have much explanatory power for my use-wear samples.

Although it was clear in many cases that a tool had been hafted, it was difficult to precisely define the limit of the haft element. Additionally, the small number of complete tools that were hafted made any comparisons of temporal resharpening indices suspect.

Neither of the above measures proposed by Odell consider use-wear features. During the analysis of the Solutré samples, it was noticed that on some retouched tools, microplating was present at the boundary between the interior tool surface and the termination of a retouch flake scar. It was obvious, though, upon closer examination that the microplating was a fragment of a once larger feature. This wear signature indicates that the tool was retouched to remove microplating that had made the tool edge ineffective, although the prehistoric user certainly did not know that microplating was the culprit. Therefore, the presence of such a wear feature indicates that a tool was resharpened and this is more likely to occur on curated tools. However, as with the resharpening index mentioned above, the sample of tools on which a use-wear signature of resharpening is present is so limited that temporal comparisons are not meaningful. I suspect that my small sample of this curation signature is due to the fact that this analysis focused on casts of ventral surfaces, and I have previously discussed the reasoning behind the focus on ventral surfaces. Only in rare instances was retouch present on the ventral surface. Had dorsal casts been made, I am sure that numerous instances of microplating being removed by means of resharpening would have been recognized since dorsal surfaces were more commonly retouched.

Hafting

Another indicator of curation is use-wear evidence related to hafting (e.g., Keeley 1982; Shott 1986). One of the components of my definition of curation is the presence of tools in the toolkit that were carried from location to location and used multiple times over a period of time. Constructing hafts and modifying tools so that they can be securely placed in a haft is a time consuming endeavor. Consequently, tools that have such an investment of time and effort associated with them are likely to be used multiple times, maintained as needed, and carried to multiple locations. Odell (1996:55) points out that this is useful when analyzing tools that have obvious haft elements (e.g., projectile points), but that this indicator is not applicable to other elements of a lithic assemblage. I think that Odell's conclusion is true when referring to low-power use-wear analyses. It is difficult, if not impossible in many instances, to recognize hafting with low-power methods if there are no macroscopic indicators of it. The Solutré assemblages include many blades and flakes that have no obvious haft elements but have microwear features, observed at high magnifications, which indicate they were hafted at one time. Therefore, one advantage of high-power use-wear methods is the ability to recognize tools that were hafted—tools that would likely be missed with low-power methods. Odell (1996:57–58) mentions that the ability to recognize a large percentage of the tools in a toolkit that were transported from location to location is extremely difficult. For hand-held tools, this is certainly true. However, if one can recognize hafted tools, then one can isolate that portion of a toolkit that had a high likelihood of being transported from location to location, and the high-power use-wear methods used in this analysis are successful at doing this.

Number of Employable Units

Another way to identify curated tools is by quantifying the number of employable units (EUs) per tool. As will be discussed later, Knudson's (1973) definition of employable unit is used in this analysis. The reason for quantifying employable units is that curated tools are likely to have a higher number of EUs than expedient tools, since they are more likely to have been transported from location to location and used multiple times. Shott (1986) compared two Paleoindian assemblages and inferred that the curated toolkit belonging to more highly mobile hunter-gatherers had a higher average of EUs per tool than the toolkit that belonged to a less mobile group.

Microplating Rounding

In the process of analyzing the Solutré samples, another likely microwear indicator of curation was recognized. As has been stated above, curated tools are more likely to be used for multiple tasks and longer periods of time than expedient tools. Consequently, one would expect microwear features to be more heavily developed on curated tools. At first, it was hypothesized that Extensively Developed Polishes or microplating would be more commonly associated with tools used for long periods of time and on multiple occasions. Experiments, however, indicated that tools used even for brief periods of time could have EDPs. It was noted, though, that the rounding of microplating over a tool's edge was a more reliable indicator of the time that a tool was used, and that tools used for long periods of time—which would be the case with curated tools—tended to have features with microplating wrapped over the tool's functional edge. As is discussed below, microplating rounding over the tool edge was quantified and recorded in the Solutré dataset.

Cleaning Strokes

Another likely indicator of curation is the presence of cleaning strokes in recorded microwear features. Cleaning strokes are created and preserved in microplating features when a finger or object is run along a tool edge to remove macroscopic debris. It is common for the user of an experimental tool, and this was likely the case in prehistory as well, to think that a decrease in tool effectiveness is due to the presence of debris on the employed edge. The examination of experimental and archaeological tools has shown that a decrease in edge efficiency is not the result of the accumulation of macroscopic debris, but rather is due to the rounding of microplating over a tool's edge. However, without the ability to view a tool edge at high magnifications, one would not know this. Therefore, the longer a tool was used, the higher the probability that debris would have built up on the tool edge and been removed thereby creating cleaning strokes. Tools with cleaning strokes are more likely to have been curated since expedient tools would have been discarded when they were no longer effective and replaced with a new tool. While it is possible that expedient tools would have had their edges cleaned of macroscopic debris during use, I assume that curated tools have a higher likelihood of having such use-wear features and therefore use the presence of cleaning strokes as a proxy indicator of curation.

Summary

One goal of this study is to determine whether the toolkits recovered from the separate cultural components were curated or expedient in their organization by examining use-wear features. In the discussion above, I have reviewed the multiple ideas of what curation means and how it can be identified in an archaeological assemblage. I have defined curation as it is used in this analysis and identified use-wear attributes that are likely indicators of curation. It is hoped that the use-wear analysis of the Solutré assemblages can determine if any of the cultural assemblages' toolkits are curated and what this may indicate with reference to site use, scheduling, raw material availability, and mobility.

TYPOLOGY AND MICROWEAR

At Solutré, we have a site with an unquestionable principal site function, multiple technologically different cultural complexes, and possible variability in secondary site functions, or minor site uses, throughout the Upper Paleolithic. With such possible variability, one might expect to see a wide range of variability with respect to tool typologies and expected tool actions. Thus, one of the analytical backdrops to the Solutré use-wear analysis is to see how its results compare to other studies that have posed questions pertaining to typology and related use-wear signatures.

Lithic analyses of Upper Paleolithic assemblages are heavily reliant on the use of typology based on tool morphology. The types defined by de Sonneville-Bordes and Perrot (1954) are still used today and are useful for ordering assemblages into groups. Typological groupings of artifacts make the variability encountered in assemblages more visible and interpretable for the archaeologist (Odell 1981b). The problem is whether or not these typological classifications are reliable indicators of how such tools were actually used (Semenov 1970).

Morphological typologies provide a comprehensive framework within which the entire range of implements found in assemblages can be inventoried (Sackett

1966:359). Bordes (1967) thought that stylistic or morphological changes in a lithic industry were the most reliable method for recognizing and studying culture change. He recognized that form and function were often related but thought functional studies could only be used to complement traditional typological studies (Bordes 1967). Semenov (1970) opposed Bordes' views. His primary interest was in studying the development of technologies and diachronic changes in lithic technologies, and he thought that typologies (morphological or functional) should not be constructed, since functional analysis was a completely separate form of archaeological analysis (Semenov 1970). Bordes and Semenov took extremely opposite positions on how to study changes in lithic industries through time.

It is my position that functional studies are necessary if we are to completely understand human technologies and human adaptation, and that the sole use of morphological typologies is not sufficient, since it is necessary to determine if the, "... functional names that have been traditionally assigned to specific lithic forms can be used to denote the actual prehistoric function(s) of individual artifacts" (Odell 1981:321). Odell (1981) points out that tool form does sometimes coincide with function, but there are a number of examples that demonstrate that current Upper Paleolithic typologies, based on tool morphology, are not always suited for identifying functional variability within tool classes.

Microwear analyses have suggested that a specific tool type was used in a variety of unexpected activities and on a variety of materials. It is possible, in some instances, that typology alone cannot be used to make determinations of tool function, and in turn, site activities and site function. Use-wear analyses, when used in conjunction with traditional technological lithic studies, can be used to make more accurate interpretations of how specific types of tools were used, and therefore lead to more precise determinations of site activities. As has been previously discussed, use-wear analyses allow us to take a chaîne opératoire study to its natural completion. Studies that are strictly typological in nature do not allow us to do this because, without use-wear, the constructed typological classifications are not functionally verified.

Odell's (1978, 1981) analysis of the assemblage from the site of Bergumermeer (Pays-Bas) demonstrates that specific morphological tool types were used in a variety of activities. There is a great deal of overlap between function and morphological tool types. For example, wear patterns from scraping are seen on knives, axes, burins, and borers. He also finds that endscrapers, sidescrapers, and burins were used in cutting activities. These results are in contrast to our traditional assumptions about tool types and function. Odell is able to demonstrate that a single function can crosscut many distinct tool classes. However, one must keep in mind that this analysis was performed without the aid of high-power magnification, so its results should be viewed with caution.

Knecht (1988:133) states that burin typologies that use the bit morphology as the primary distinguishing characteristic of type are based on the idea that the bit is the functional portion of the burin. Her analysis of burin polishes indicates that burin facets were oftentimes the functional portion of the tool and may have been used in a variety of motions on a variety of worked materials.

Barton et al. (1996) use macroscopic edge damage and retouch to challenge the idea that burins are a distinct class of tool. They conclude that many burin types do not represent distinct classes of tools. Rather, they are a result of technical aspects of manufacture and the effects of use and maintenance (Barton et al. 1996). One must call into question their results since they used macroscopic damage and low magnification analyses to arrive at their conclusions. Such magnification levels do not, in my mind, allow unequivocal conclusions of tool use because numerous influences other than tool use (i.e. post-depositional processes) can leave traces which could mislead a use-wear analyst. Post-depositional wear traces are more easily discerned at higher magnifications.

Vaughan's (1990) analysis of the Mesolithic artifacts from Franchthi cave also found that there was little correspondence between tool morphology and use action. He attributes this lack of correspondence to the fact that the toolkit was expedient meaning that any appropriate tool edge was used for a specific task without regard to overall tool form (Vaughan 1990:252). Related to this, is his finding that only one third of the tools showed more than one utilized portion of the tool edge (Vaughan 1990:252). It is possible that this lack of correspondence between typology and tool function is more common in tool assemblages that are primarily expedient in nature. So too, this result must be evaluated with caution.

Contrary to these above examples is an analysis of stone tools from Klithi (Moss 1997). Moss (1997:193) found that typological categories corresponded well with their anticipated functions. Scrapers were used in scraping activities, the lateral edges of blades and flakes were used to cut, backed bladelets (the anticipated hunting component of the toolkit) were used as projectiles, and that microperçoirs were used to bore.

Keeley's (1988) analysis of three Magdalenian assemblages has similar typological and functional results to those of Moss (1997). His study of stone tools from Verberie, Rascano, and El Juyo, demonstrates that morphological and typological categories corresponded well with their anticipated functions.

Numerous use-wear studies, utilizing a variety of magnifications and microscopes, have suggested that a single morphological tool type was used to perform a number of different functions (e.g., Barton et al. 1996; Knecht 1988; Odell 1978, 1981), that multiple morphological forms were used to fulfill the same function (e.g., Semenov 1964), and that typological classes were used in the manner that archaeologists anticipate and did not deviate from those functions (i.e., scrapers used to scrape, blades used to cut, burins used to groove, etc.) (e.g., Keeley 1988; Moss 1997).

One goal of this use-wear analysis of the Solutré assemblages is to determine if a priori assumptions of typology and function are correct in this site specific case, or if there are significant deviations between typology and function. A microwear analysis that examines use-generated polishes, as well as multiple tool motion indicators (i.e., striations, abrasive particle placement, presence and placement of crystallization filaments), can lead to an understanding of how tools with specific morphological forms were used. This issue was evaluated during the examination and interpretation of the tools that composed this study's samples.

CHAPTER 6: DATABASE AND WEAR FEATURE CODING

As was discussed in the previous chapter, the primary goals of this microwear analysis are: 1) to determine if there are significant differences in the overall use-wear signatures between the major Upper Paleolithic cultural components at Solutré, 2) to determine if there is any correlation between typology and assumed function for the samples from each cultural component; and, 3) to determine which toolkits from the cultural components have a use-wear signature thought to be indicative of "curation" and explain any potential variability with respect to mobility and raw material availability.

In order to carry out the analysis of the use-wear data with these goals in mind, it was necessary to create two databases in order to examine the results. The first database is focused on the individual artifact and was more focused on tool function and typology. The second database is structured so that each employable unit's (EU, discussed in detail below) attributes are the focus of analysis, and its structure is geared towards examining curation signatures. The reason for creating this second EU database is that the initial artifact-oriented database's organization prevents it from being effectively queried during many attempted assemblage comparisons that are focused on the number and types of EUs for each tool. The two databases contain the same information and the only difference between the two is one of organization. The artifact-oriented database has the EUs described in multiple columns in the same data row, whereas the EU-focused database gives each tool EU its own row. As stated above, the information contained in the artifact database does not differ from the EU database, but rather each artifact has its own data row and each artifact's EU(s) and corresponding data (e.g., EU#, edge angle, use identification, etc.) was given a block of columns in that row.

To create these databases, the folders of use-wear notes and feature descriptions, artifact drawings, and photomicrographs for each artifact were reviewed. Wear feature photomicrographs and written descriptions were compared with experimentally produced wear feature photomicrographs to verify or refine the preliminary determination of use action and worked material made at the time of examination. In some instances, no definitive determination of worked material was made at the time of microscopic examination. These indeterminate features were closely compared to the experimental image database in an attempt to make a determination of worked material. There are some EUs for which the worked material remains indeterminate and in some rare instances artifact motion or use identification is also indeterminate.

Employable Units

In order to quantify distinct and functionally, and oftentimes physically, different areas of use on a single tool, Knudson's (1979:270) concept of employable unit (EU) is used. Knudson defines an EU as the following:

"An EU [employable unit] is conceptually defined as that segment or portion (an edge, projection, facial arris, or facial surface) of an implement when that implement is used against another material to perform a task (e.g., cutting, scraping, drilling, etc.). The unit is usually identified as that part of a tool edge bounded by abrupt changes in plan contour, or the conjunction of two edges and surfaces where the conjunction (projection) itself becomes the point of work force application. An EU's identification as a potentially culturally significant unit is the presence of deliberate piece or edge thinning flake scars (retouch) and/or apparent postproduction modification (edge spalling, striae, abrasion, polish, etc.)" (1979:270).

In many instances a single episode of use on a single worked material can create physically separated areas of wear, and directionality indicators and/or identical polish attributes resulted in the coding of a single EU. In instances where it could be determined that one edge, or tool portion, had been used to work materials of differing hardness and with a different use motion or action (e.g. cutting versus scraping), two EUs were coded for that tool due to the use of one edge to fulfill multiple and functionally distinct roles. Finally, it is not uncommon in the Solutré assemblages to see tools that have mostly separate but slightly overlapping EUs. Such patterns tend to occur when a tool has EUs on both its lateral and end portions. An example is a broken blade with cutting wear features that run along the tool edge up to the edge's intersection with the break and burin on break use (coded as burin 2 use) along said intersection and the break.

Each EU is coded for motion of tool use (useid) and worked material hardness (categ). When comparisons to experimental images produced a match to specific material type (wood, soft plant, bone/antler), it is noted in the notes column. In many instances, though, one can only remain confident at the level of hardness identification, and because many EUs lacked specificity with respect to material type, all comparisons discussed later will remain at the level of worked material hardness.

Tool Motion Codes

With respect to tool motion, cutting is coded when the wear features do not definitively match with butchery experiments related to disarticulation and could have been produced by cutting soft materials in a non-butchery context. Most cutting wear features, though, are likely related to animal processing at some stage since they resemble hide cutting or meat filleting: butchery activities in which contact with dense or hard animal materials is unlikely. The fact that animal processing was one of the principal site activities throughout the Upper Paleolithic supports such coding. Butchery is coded in instances where the wear features show evidence of soft material contact as well as medium and/or hard material contact, and the polish attributes and directionality indicators on such wear features match with the experimental butchery tools. (Appendix B-1, B-2).

The scraping code is assigned when striations are predominantly oriented perpendicular to the working edge, or parallel to tool motion, and directionality indicators (i.e. trapped abrasives, crystallization filaments) indicate a motion from the interior of the tool towards the working edge (Figure 8). Planing is coded when the same suite of attributes occurred but motion is from the edge to the interior of the tool. Planing is also coded when back and forth motion was evident since the planing and scraping experiments demonstrate that planing produces back and forth wear more consistently (Figure 9). The reason behind this is that oftentimes during planing actions the working edge is not completely lifted off the worked material when the working edge is being repositioned for another planing motion.

Wear patterns indicating work on hard materials, typically bone or antler, are coded with three different codes. The burin code is used when burin wear is present on the bit and dihedrals of a bit on a formal burin. Burin wear is typically restricted to the edge and characterized by numerous, densely packed striations and numerous abrasive particles (Figures 10 and 11). The burin 2 code is used when the same type of wear is observed on the break and/or corner of a break on a broken tool, blade, or flake, and the tool cannot be coded as a formal burin (Figures 12 and 13). Finally, the grooving code is used when similar wear signatures are observed on a tool edge but are more invasive than typical burin or burin 2 wear (Figure 14). The invasive nature of the polish is a result of the working edge being placed in a pre-existing groove in the processed bone or antler and used in a sawing motion. Examples of these can be seen in the experimental tools used to deepen grooves along the spines of soaked bison scapulae in order to facilitate their removal.

Worked Material Hardness Codes

Three broad categories of worked material hardness codes are used, and there are finer subdivisions within each category. The first principal category is soft. This is assigned to features that are invasive and do not have the blocky attributes or densely packed striations associated with medium and hard materials, respectively. This code represents the polish features described for soft materials in the discussion of experimental tools in Chapter 4. The soft-medium code is used when features related to working soft material also exhibit attributes indicative of infrequent contact with materials of medium hardness during what appears to be the same use episode. This most typically occurs during butchery when cartilage is contacted on an infrequent basis. The soft-hard code is used when the same as described above is the case except the minor component of the wear features is characteristic of contact with hard material. This also typically occurred during the butchery experiments when limbs were disarticulated or muscle units were disconnected from bone. Features indicative of work on woods, both soft and hard woods as well as green and dry woods, are assigned the medium code. This code is assigned to the features described in Chapter 4 pertaining to experimental work performed on a variety of woods. The medium-hard category is assigned when work on wood is the dominant signature, but there are some indications that harder material was contacted during use and it cannot definitively be ascertained that these were separate use episodes on the same EU. In such instances it is also possible that dry woods were worked, and the lack of moisture in the wood resulted in wear features that correspond well with features observed in the wood working experiments but also had attributes typically observed in features attributable to harder materials.

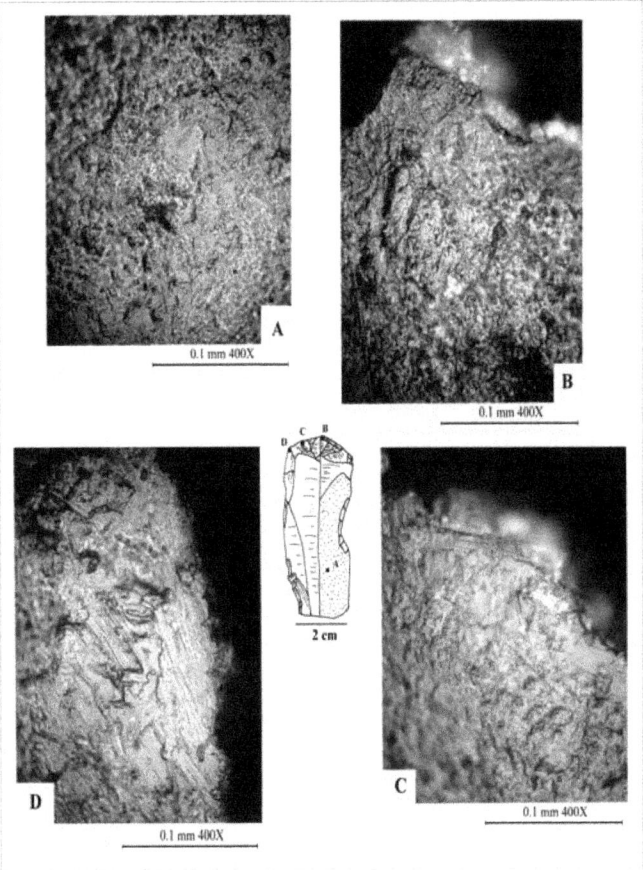

Figure 8: *M12 Est Au1 WEB 5 – scraping, hard contact.*

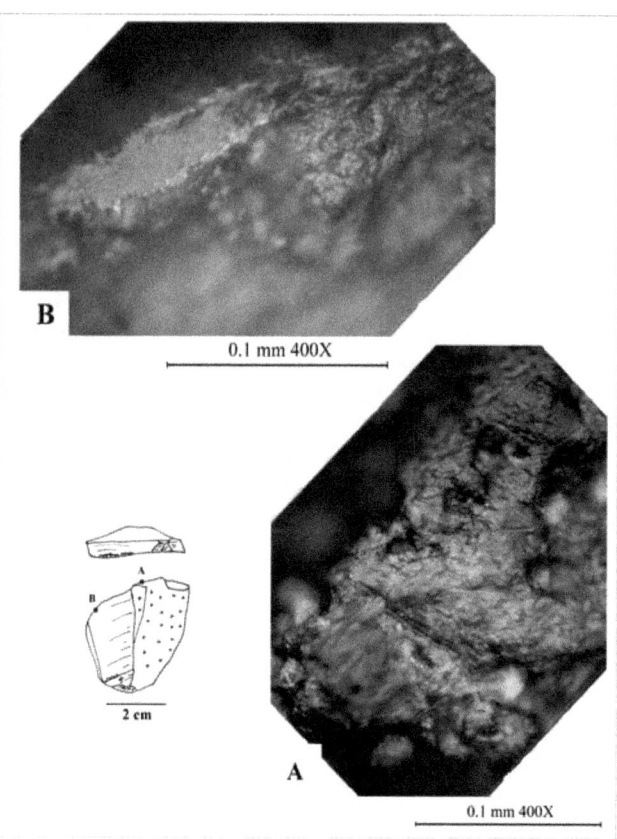

Figure 9: L13 WEB 901 – *planing.*

Finally, the code "hard" is assigned to the types of wear features seen on tools used to work either bone or antler. These feature attributes have been previously described in the burin code discussion above and the experimental descriptions in Chapter 4.

For the statistical comparisons described later, the hard category could not be analyzed at its finer subdivisions due to the wide range of coded features. This range of variability made statistical comparisons at more specific levels invalid because the sample sizes were too small. Therefore, all hardness comparisons between time periods are conducted at the level of the broader categories (i.e. soft, medium, and hard). For these comparisons, the codes that are a combination of hardness (e.g. soft-hard, medium-hard) are placed in the broad category of the softest material in the hardness combination. For example, EUs assigned a soft-hard code are placed in the broad category of soft for the statistical comparisons. This is done because the first material hardness code in such a combination is the dominant hardness signature.

Other Coded Wear Feature Attributes

A number of other wear feature attributes are coded, although they occur at much lower frequencies than the motion and material hardness attributes, and they are described below. These attributes are used in later comparisons of the degree of curation/expediency of the lithic assemblages. The concept of curation and the definition of (or attributes of) curation used for this study were discussed in Chapter 5.

Edge Rounding

The first of these attributes that is a proxy measure of the degree of curation is edge rounding. The defined EUs, and their associated wear features, exhibit a wide range of variability of rounding over their respective tool edges. Rounding variability was coded as either none, minor, moderate, and well. The experimental program associated with this study has shown that the degree of edge rounding is a reliable proxy measure of the intensity of tool use. Tools used only briefly have features that are restricted to the tool's surface and do not wrap over the tool edge. When such features are observed, the EU's rounding is coded as none. The experimental tools used for intermediate lengths of time exhibit two primary types of edge rounding: minor and moderate. For this study, minor edge rounding is coded when a wear feature is primarily restricted to the tool's surface with very small projections of polish that have begun to wrap over the tool edge, but the unaltered tool edge is still clearly visible. Moderate edge rounding is coded when a polish has completely wrapped over the tool edge, but the natural form of the edge is still clearly discernible underneath the wrapped polish. The last rounding category is "well". This is coded when a polish is so extensively wrapped over the tool edge that the natural form of the edge can no longer be discerned. This occurs on tools that have been used for extensive periods of time and the edge is no longer effective due to the extensive polish rounding. Experimental tools used for extended periods without any resharpening routinely exhibit such rounding. For assemblage comparisons, this attribute is viewed at the level of the artifact and not individual EUs. For tools that have multiple EUs, and therefore multiple rounding codes, the most well-developed EU rounding code is assigned to that artifact.

One might think that documenting the frequencies of occurrence for weakly, intermediately, and extensively developed polishes would be another means to measure the intensity of tool use for use as a proxy measure of curation. However, experiments have shown this to not be the case, and indicate that edge rounding is a more reliable indicator of the intensity of tool use. The reason behind this are the observations on experimental tools that even brief periods of use (ca. 15–30 minutes) can produce extensively developed polishes, but the microplating events are restricted to the tool's surface and the edges have either no edge rounding or minor rounding. It is possible that the intensity of microplating expression is related to the moisture content of the worked material and not necessarily related to the intensity of use (M. Kay 2004, personal communication). However, the length of use is certainly a factor in the

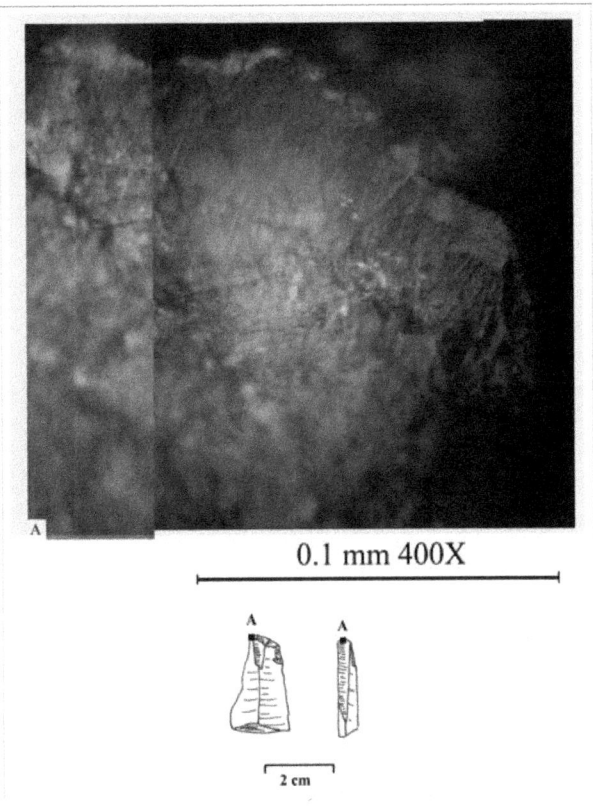

Figure 10: P16u14 – burin wear.

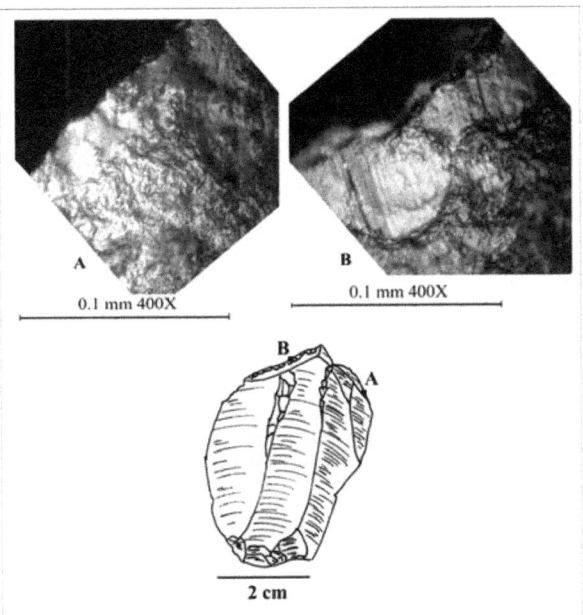

Figure 11: I11u78-487 – burin wear.

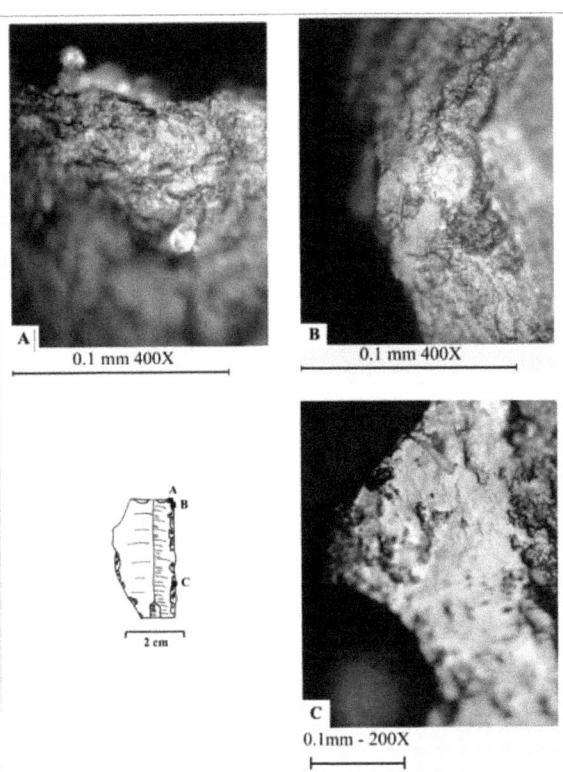

Figure 12: P16u58-198 – burin 2 wear.

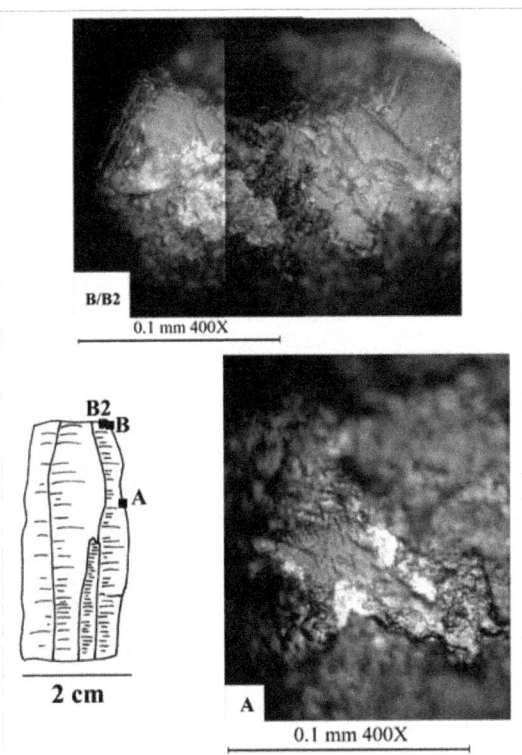

Figure 13: J10 WEB11 – burin 2 wear.

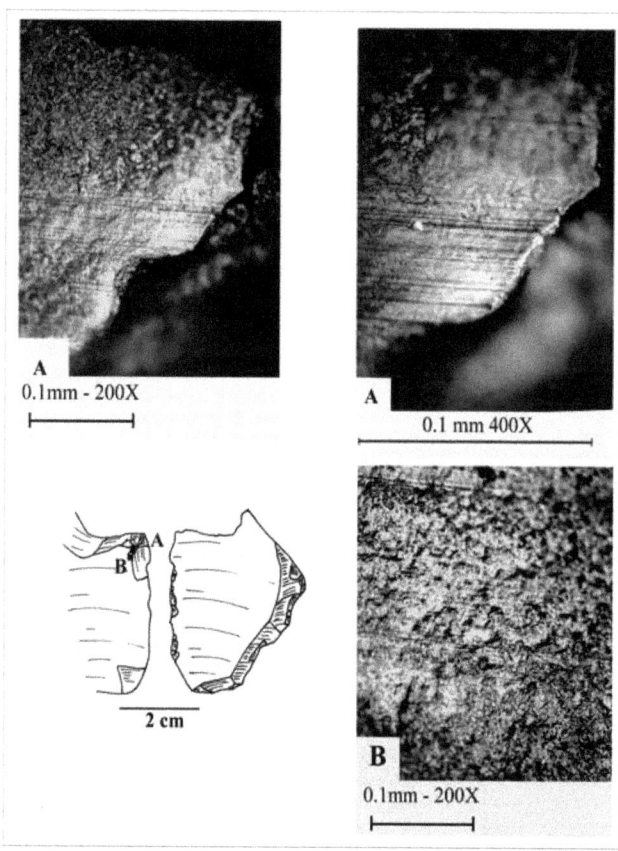

Figure 14: P16u68-490 – grooving wear.

degree to which microplating is wrapped over a tool's edge. It is for this reason that the degree of edge rounding, and not polish development, is used as a measure of the intensity of tool use.

Presence of Cleaning Strokes

Another attribute that is coded, but unfortunately occurs in low frequencies, is the presence of a cleaning stroke, or strokes, incorporated into a polish or polishes along a tool edge. These are primarily seen on tools that exhibit well rounded polished edges, although in some instances they are present along edges over which polishes are moderately rounded. As the experimental evidence has shown, additive polishes are the most common type of wear. While abrasive wear does occur, it is most often an expression of a previous microplating event that has undergone abrasion as tool use is prolonged. Experiments have also shown that as tool use continues, and the tool edge is not manually resharpened or rejuvenated, microplating increases in its extent and thickness, eventually wrapping over the tool edge and completely obscuring it. These thick deposits of microplating on the tool edge serve to round it and make it a non-functional edge. Throughout the preliminary analyses of the Solutré assemblage, and in discussion with Marvin Kay of the University of Arkansas relating to the patterns he has seen on archaeological tools, it was noted that many extensively developed microplating events that exhibit moderate to well-rounded edges have long, deep, and typically broad striations that run parallel to the tool's working edge (Figure 15). Kay (1998) had previously interpreted these to be the by-products of attempts to manually clean the tool edge. As discussed in Chapter 4, the experimental program reproduced this particular polish attribute with some success by using tools to exhaustion and attempting to refresh an edge by simply pinching it and running one's fingers along the edge to remove the visible debris which had built up along the edge. To the naked eye, the edge appeared to still be sharp and functional, but as the experimental tools have shown, microplating has made the edge non-functional when examined at a microscopic level. Such scenarios demonstrate the power of high-power use-wear examinations. One is able to recognize used and likely discarded tools that would go unrecognized in examinations using only the naked eye. The frequency of cleaning strokes is also considered to be a proxy measure of where an assemblage sits on the conceptual continuum between curation and expediency. If a tool was considered by its users to be "expedient", then one would expect to see either brief use as indicated by minor microplating development and either no cleaning strokes or a very low frequency of cleaning strokes. Tools that were used extensively and show extensively developed microplating have a higher probability of having belonged to a more curated toolkit, and because they were used longer, have a higher probability of exhibiting cleaning attempts in their microplating events.

Hafting and Prehension Wear

The last minor attribute that is coded, when adequate use-wear evidence is visible, is the determination of whether or not a tool was hand-held or hafted. This too helps in determining the degree to which a cultural assemblage is curated. While this study's experimental program did not include any hafted tools, there are examples in Marvin Kay's experimental photomicrograph collection at the University of Arkansas. There are also numerous published accounts that document the characteristics and variability of hafting wear traces as seen with Nomarski optics (Banks 2002b; Kay 1996, 1998, 2000). Since such wear is described in detail elsewhere, its characteristic attributes will only be summarized below.

Hafting wear can be abrasive or additive in nature, and oftentimes exists as a combination of both. When haft wear is strictly abrasive in nature, it is usually expressed as abrasive planing. This has been previously described as a large smooth area that is highly reflective and represents an area where the tool's higher microtopography has been planed smooth. Oftentimes, there are fine and shallow striations present on the surface of the planed surface.

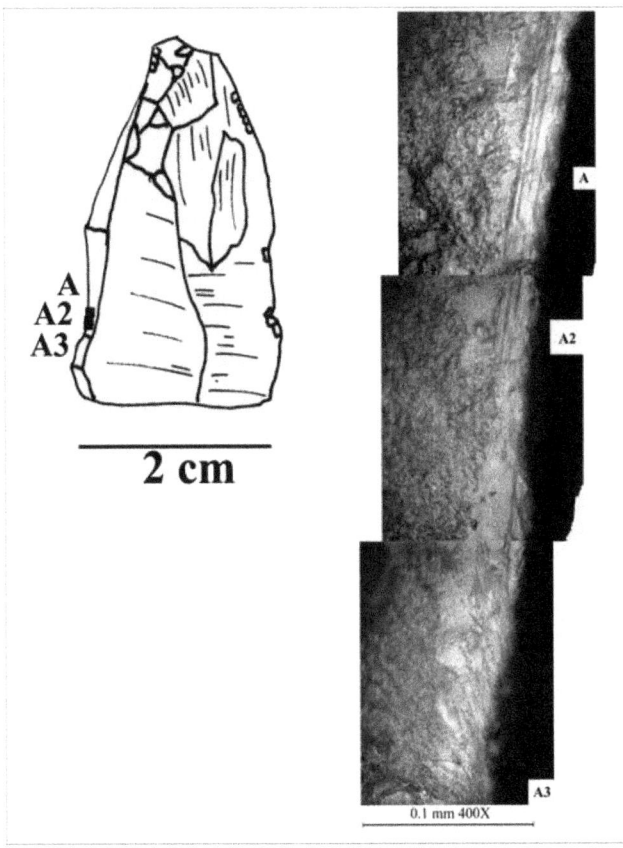

Figure 15: L13hh – cleaning stroke example.

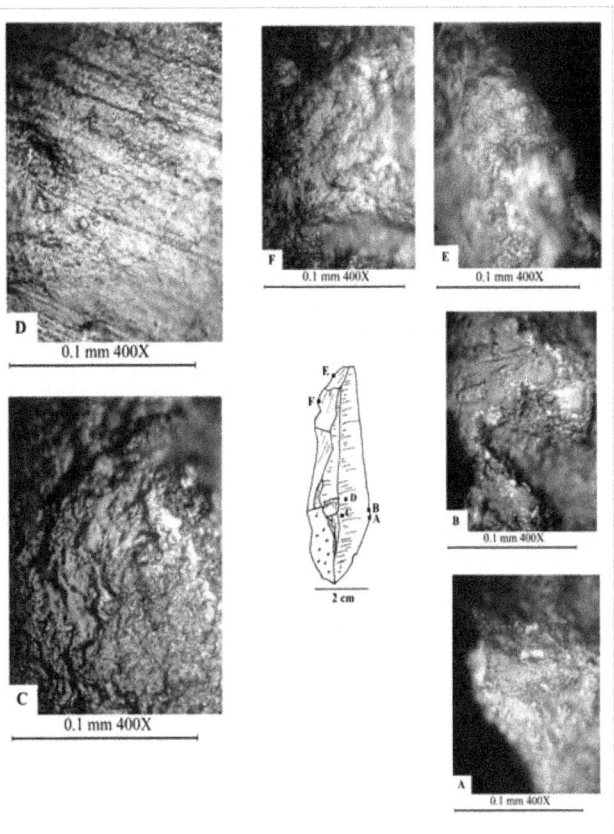

Figure 16: L13g WEB1 – hafting wear.

When hafting wear is expressed as microplating, the microwear is almost always expressed as an EDP and striations are commonly medium to broad in width with either a rounded or rectangular cross section (Figure 16). Also, the striation sets commonly form a lattice pattern meaning that they are oriented perpendicular to one another. It is also common to see this lattice pattern intersected with obliquely oriented sets of striations. This intersecting pattern of striations results from the back and forth movement of the tool within the haft element. Another common attribute of haft wear is spot crystallization. As was described in Chapter 4, the back and forth movement of a tool will take the crystallization that forms on a polishes trailing edge and reincorporate into the microplating event as it is formed.

The final type of hafting wear is microplating, with some or all of the characteristics described above, that has begun to be abraded. The polish has begun to take on an abraded appearance but the remnants of the microplating event's attributes are still visible, although muted.

Prehension traces tend to occur as abrasive weakly developed polishes that may exhibit faint striations (Figure 17). These abrasive WDPs tend to be small in size and are isolated or localized in nature, meaning that there are generally no other traces of use in their immediate vicinity.

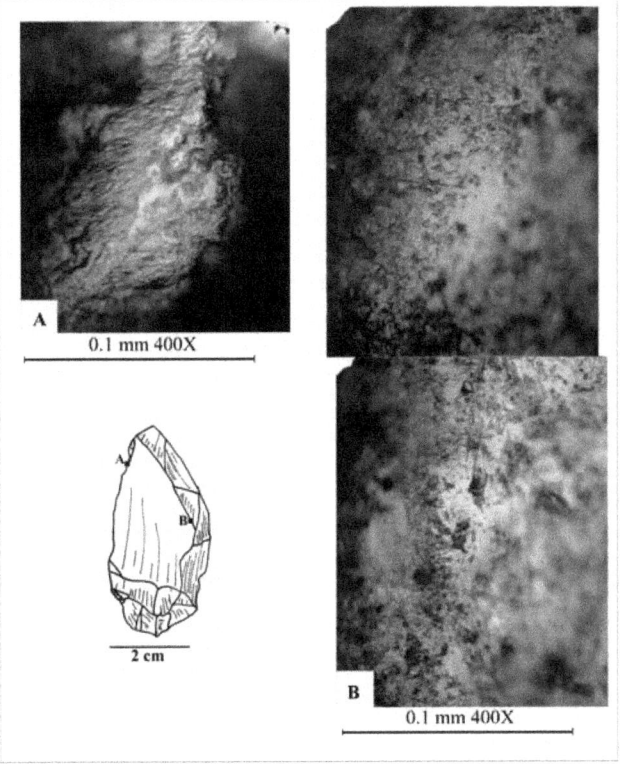

Figure 17: J10u27-2 – prehension.

CHAPTER 7: ANALYSIS

The dense bonebeds recorded during both old and modern excavations, the presence of hunting weaponry, and the evidence of butchery on many recovered faunal elements all clearly demonstrate that Solutré was principally used as a location to intercept and dispatch large game animals during the Upper Paleolithic. Despite these commonalities, there are differences in the composition of the lithic assemblages recovered from the different cultural levels. The Aurignacian assemblages are relatively lithic poor, the Gravettian components are dominated by blades, the Solutrean has a wide variety of specialized and general purpose tools, and the Magdalenian toolkit is diverse and typologically specialized. This variability hints at possible differences in secondary site activities between the time periods, and potential differences in how Solutré was incorporated in settlement systems and resource acquisition schedules through time. A variety of use-wear attributes and metric variables are examined with a number of different statistical methods in this Chapter in an effort to identify and quantify any possible differences.

CHI-SQUARE COMPARISONS

Tool Motion or Use Action

One of the goals of this study is to identify possible differences in secondary site function or activities that might exist between the cultural components. Because the determinations of tool action and worked material are not continuous variables, the chi-square statistic is used to determine if the observed variability between the assemblages is significant.

Thomas (1986:283) quotes Leslie A. White, "A device that explains everything explains nothing", to suggest that while chi-square tests can be informative, they are often misused in the anthropological literature and the interpretation of this statistic is difficult. While this is true, if the value of each cell's contribution to the final chi-square statistic is taken into consideration, along with graphical plots of the data, one can attain a good understanding of which cells in the contingency table are influencing a statistically significant result.

The first chi-square statistic is the comparison of use action by time period. Earlier, the codes assigned for use action were described, and it was noted that many of the minor, but similar, action subdivisions had to be combined for this comparison. If all of the action assignments are kept separate for the time period comparisons, the chi-square statistic is invalid because there are too many empty or low value cells in the contingency table. Therefore, cutting and butchery actions are combined under the heading of butchery. The scraping category includes both scraping and planing codes. The burin group includes the codes of burin, burin 2, and grooving. This comparison is conducted at the level of the EU rather than the individual artifact so that the complete range of tool actions for each time period is accounted for, and these data are contained in Table 2. The chi-square statistic calculated for this contingency table ($X^2 = 45.57$, d.f. = 6, $\alpha = 0.05$, $p < 0.001$) is significant, thus allowing the null hypothesis of no difference to be rejected. The causes of the statistically significant result are numerous. The primary contributors are the high observed frequency of butchery activities represented in the Gravettian assemblage (Figure 18) and the Gravettian assemblage's low frequency of scraping and planing actions, in relation to the expected frequency. These differences contribute to roughly half of the calculated statistic. Thus, the Gravettian assemblage is focused on butchery and related processing activities. The secondary contributors to the rejection of the null hypothesis are the low frequency of butchery activities and high frequency of burin type actions in the Magdalenian assemblage. The frequencies associated with butchery and scraping activities in the Aurignacian assemblage are possible but distant contributors. The Aurignacian has a slightly lower than expected frequency of butchery activities, and a slightly higher than expected frequency of scraping activities. The Solutrean assemblage's observed and expected frequencies show almost no difference for each broad category of use action and do not contribute to the significant chi-square result.

Table 2: General use action counts for employable units.

$X^2_{alpha = 0.05, 6} = 45.57$; $p < 0.001$

Time Period	Butchery	Scraping	Burin	Total
Aurignacian	11	23	4	38
Gravettian	44	7	3	54
Solutrean	10	13	2	25
Magdalenian	7	18	9	34
Total	72	61	18	151

In order to visually depict this significant use action variability, the percentages of each use action, with respect to each time period's total EU sample, were plotted and are depicted in Figure 19. While percentages of use action are not the same as the observed frequencies, calculating percentages allows the observed frequencies to be roughly normalized, and the graphic results mirror the statistical results detailed above. The EUs associated with butchery actions account for over 80% of the EUs recorded in the Gravettian assemblage. The Gravettian EU sample also deviates significantly from the other cultural components with respect to scraping and planing tool actions. This graphic variation of the Gravettian use actions supports the statistics that show these deviations account for nearly 50% of the chi-square value. This graphic representation of use action percentages also accurately depicts the statistical results associated with the Aurignacian EUs. One notes the low percentage of butchery actions and the high percentage of scraping and planing actions. With respect to scraping and planing, the Solutrean and Magdalenian samples are essentially identical. With the exception of the Magdalenian sample, all time periods are nearly identical when it comes to the percentage of burin related actions. The Magdalenian burin EUs occur at a higher frequency with respect to the other cultural components.

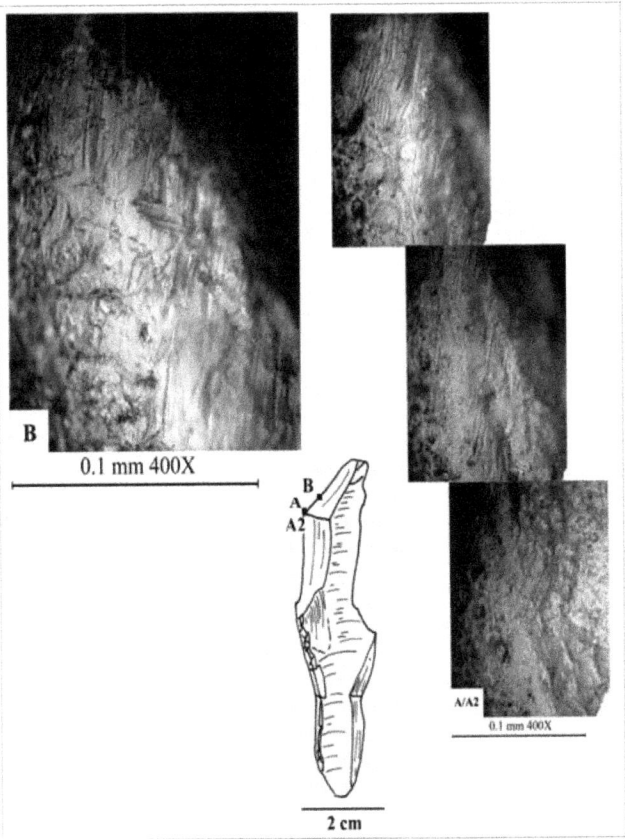

Figure 18: L13k WEB18 – butchery wear.

The results of this use action comparison fit well with the observed characteristics of the recovered lithic assemblages. The Gravettian is dominated by retouched and unretouched blades, and has relatively few formal tools in comparison to the other time periods. This is a composition that one would expect in an assemblage geared towards butchery and initial carcass processing. A wide range of formal tool types dominates the Magdalenian tool assemblage. With such a wide range of tool types, one would expect there to be a significant amount of use actions not directly related to butchery or carcass processing. A similar situation is true for the Aurignacian assemblage. While it tends to be lithic poor, and less dominated by formal tools than the Magdalenian, there is a higher frequency of formal tool types relative to the Gravettian assemblage, and it is not surprising to see activities other than primary butchery and carcass processing represented.

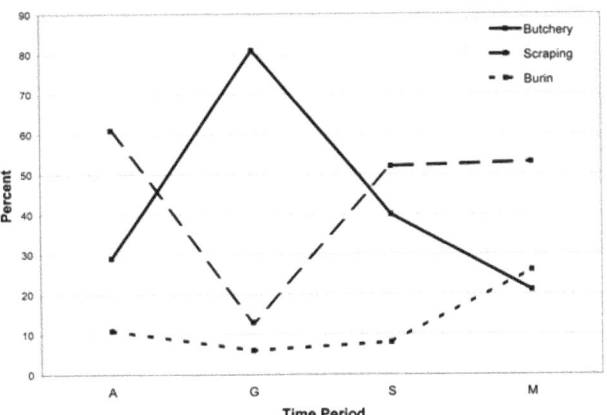

Figure 19: Use action percentages by time period.

Worked Material

The next chi-square test evaluates the frequencies of worked material hardness at the level of the employable unit. As was the case with use action, the finer categories of hardness had to be combined into coarser groups so that a valid chi-square statistic could be calculated. The first of the broad groups is "soft" which includes the soft, soft–medium, and soft–hard codes. The medium category includes the medium and medium–hard classes. The last category represents wear features resulting from contact with hard contact materials. The resultant observed frequencies are contained in Table 3. The calculated chi-square statistic ($X^2 = 31.07$, d.f = 6, $\alpha = 0.05$, $p < 0.001$) for this contingency table is significant. When reviewing the contributing chi-square contributions from each cell of the contingency table, one can identify the hardness category and time period cells that cause this significant result. In contrast to the previous comparison, the Magdalenian assemblage accounts for much of the significant variability in this statistical comparison (ca. 33%). The primary Magdalenian contributors are the high observed frequency of hard contact materials and the low frequency of soft contact materials with respect to the calculated expected frequencies. This corresponds with the use action frequencies showing lower than expected butchery and higher than expected frequencies of burin and grooving actions in the Magdalenian sample. Again, as was the case with the use action statistical comparison, the Gravettian assemblage accounts for much of significant variability between observed and expected frequencies. This significant variability is marked by a high frequency of soft contact materials (butchery) and a low frequency of hard contact materials (burin related actions). The minor contributors to this significant chi-square statistics are the lower than expected frequency of soft contact materials in the Aurignacian assemblage and the lower than expected frequency of hard contact materials in the Solutrean assemblage. However, these calculations are so low that they most likely do not contribute to the significant result.

As would be expected, the worked material patterns closely resemble the use action patterns discussed previously.

Table 3: Worked material hardness counts for employable units.

Time Period	Soft	Medium	Hard	Total
Aurignacien	16	17	14	47
Gravettian	40	14	5	59
Solutrean	24	10	3	37
Magdalenian	12	15	18	45
Total	92	56	40	188

$X^2_{alpha = 0.05, 6} = 31.07; p < 0.001$

As was done with the use action data, the worked material hardness counts were converted to percentages and graphed. The line graph (Figure 20) illustrates the significant results with only one erroneous graphic placement. The soft category for the Solutrean assemblage appears to be significant when the percentages are viewed graphically. However, the statistical calculations demonstrate that this is not the case.

Hafting/Prehension

The frequencies of hafting and prehension microwear traces are evaluated to see if there is significant variability between the cultural components. This contingency table is depicted in Table 4. Unlike the previous comparisons, which were conducted at the level of the EU, this statistic is calculated with the artifact as the basis of comparison. The calculated chi-square statistic ($X2 = 18.51$, d.f = 3, $\alpha = 0.05$, $p < 0.001$) is significant. The greatest contributors to this significant
chi-square result are the higher than expected frequency of hafted tools in the Aurignacian assemblage and the lower than expected frequency of hafted tools in the Gravettian sample. Related to these patterns, and consistent with the patterns seen in previous comparisons, are the secondary contributors. These are the higher than expected frequency of hand-held tools in the Gravettian sample and the higher than expected frequency of hafted tools in the Magdalenian. Another contributor is the lower than expected frequency of hand-held tools in the Aurignacian sample, but one must view this with some skepticism since there is only one tool in the sample that had identifiable traces of prehension. Figure 21 graphically depicts the percentages calculated for this contingency table, and the patterns closely parallel the calculated statistical results. It should be noted that the hafted tool samples are small, and one might question the comparisons between the Aurignacian sample and the other time periods. Nonetheless, the Aurignacian components are relatively lithic poor, so the Aurignacian computation may be accurate.

Table 4: Hafting and prehension wear for employable units.

	Aurig.	Grav.	Solutrean	Magd.	Total
Hand	1	30	18	6	55
Haft	7	7	13	11	38
Total	8	37	31	17	93

$X^2_{alpha = 0.05, 3} = 18.51; p < 0.001$

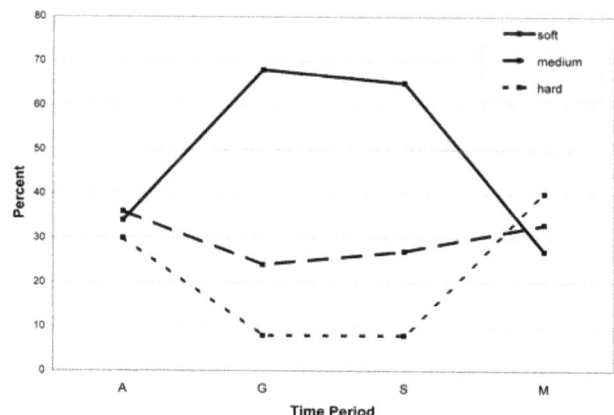

Figure 20: Hardness percentages by time period.

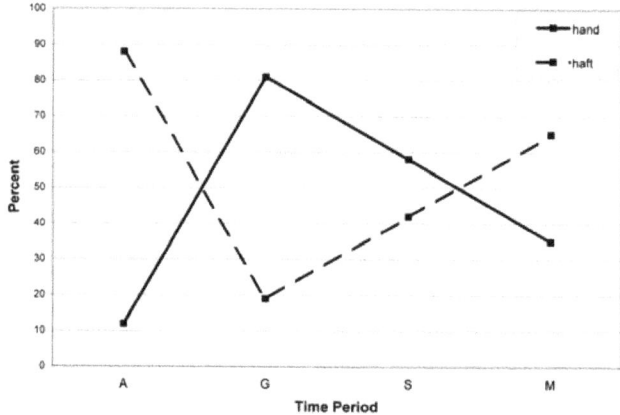

Figure 21: Hafting and prehension percentages by time period.

Edge Rounding

The final chi-square statistic comparison between time periods is concerned with the degree of edge rounding. As is the case with hafting and prehension, this contingency table (Table 5) is based at the level of the individual artifact rather than the EU. The "none" code is excluded because if it is included, the chi-square comparison is not valid due to low observed and expected cell counts. When calculated, the chi-square statistic ($X^2 = 9.415$, d.f = 6, $\alpha = 0.05$, $0.10 < p < 0.25$) is not significant; the null hypothesis is accepted. While not statistically significant, the two principal contributors to the calculated statistic are the higher than expected frequency of minor edge rounding and the lower than expected frequency of moderate rounding in the Aurignacian assemblage. The other cells in the contingency table only have minor variations between the observed and expected rounding frequencies. Therefore, the chi-square comparison of edge rounding does not point to one cultural assemblage being used more intensively, and therefore considered to be more curated, than the others.

Table 5: Degree of edge rounding counts for employable units.

Time Period	Minor	Moderate	Well	Total
Aurignacian	15	7	6	28
Gravettian	12	20	12	44
Solutrean	5	12	3	20
Magdalenian	10	16	10	36
Total	42	55	31	128

$X^2_{alpha = 0.05, 6} = 9.415; 0.10 < p < 0.25$

ANOVA RESULTS

A number of continuous variables are recorded for each artifact and employable unit. Standard metric attributes are recorded for each artifact and each EU has an associated edge angle measurement. These measurements are examined to identify any possible differences in tool use over time. The Analysis of Variance (ANOVA) - GT2 method (Sokal and Rohlf 1995:244, 248–249) is used to compare the variances of these measurements with respect to use action and worked material for each cultural sample. Once the statistic is calculated, the upper and lower limits of the variance for each class are calculated and depicted graphically. If the upper and lower limits associated with separate means overlap, they are statistically the same. If they do not overlap, the null hypothesis of no difference can be rejected.

Tool Motion or Use Action and Edge Angle Variability

When the GT2-method ANOVA comparisons of the butchery and cutting actions and their associated EU edge angles are compared for the principal time periods, it is observed that there is considerable variability (Figure 22). The Solutrean time period has the lowest average edge angle and is significantly different from all other time periods. Likewise, the Aurignacian is significantly different from the other cultural complexes but has a slightly higher average edge angle. The Gravettian and Magdalenian assemblages have higher than average edge angles than the other two time periods and are statistically the same.

With respect to the scraping and planing activities, as would be expected, the average edge angle is higher than that observed with butchery and cutting activities. The Aurignacian, Gravettian, and Magdalenian variances are all statistically the same, while the Solutrean sample's edge angle is statistically lower.

Finally, the burin edge angles for burin related activities for all time periods are all statistically the same. Surprisingly, they exhibit a wide range of variability and overlap the ranges all the time periods' scraping samples and the Gravettian and Magdalenian butchery samples.

When these limits are organized by time period and then use action (Figure 23), one notes that edge angles increase within each time period with respect to use action, and that only in the Solutrean sample are all edge angles by use action category significantly different.

Worked Material and Edge Angle Variability

When edge angle variances and worked material hardness are examined with a GT2-method ANOVA, some patterns are evident (Figure 24). First, as one would expect, there is a general increase in the average edge angle measurement as worked material hardness increases. This pattern exists because high angle edges are stronger than low angle edges and hold up better when working harder contact materials. Low angle edges deteriorate quickly when in contact with medium and hard materials. Likewise, low angle edges are more efficient for processing soft materials than higher angle edges. It is interesting to note that the average edge angle associated with soft contact materials in the Magdalenian assemblage is significantly larger than the edge angle averages of the other time periods. The Magdalenian soft edge angle average is in the range associated with medium contact materials for all the time periods, and in fact exceeds the medium material edge angle average in the Magdalenian sample, although not significantly. When these results are grouped by time period rather than hardness (Figure 25), one notes a significant difference between the average edge angles for the different worked material classes within each time period in most instances. The exceptions to this pattern are seen in the Aurignacian and Magdalenian samples. In the Aurignacian sample, the edge angle variances of the soft and medium hardness categories are statistically the same. In the Magdalenian sample, there is very little variability between the hardness classes, and only the means of the medium and hard categories are statistically different. Also, the average edge angle regardless of material hardness is relatively high.

Hafting/Prehension and Edge Angle Variability

The variability of EU edge angles for tools that could be identified as being hafted or hand-held is depicted in Figures 26 and 27. The GT2 method (ANOVA) is used to calculate upper and lower limits, which are graphically represented in the figures. The hafted tools have EUs with a relatively high average edge angle for each time period. One notes that there is a large range of variability within each temporal sample, and all of the time periods are statistically the same.

Nearly the opposite is true when hand-held tools and EU edge angles are compared. The Aurignacian is not considered in this comparison because only one tool in that sample had clear prehension wear. The average edge angle is lower than that observed for the hafted tools, and there is little variability within each sample.

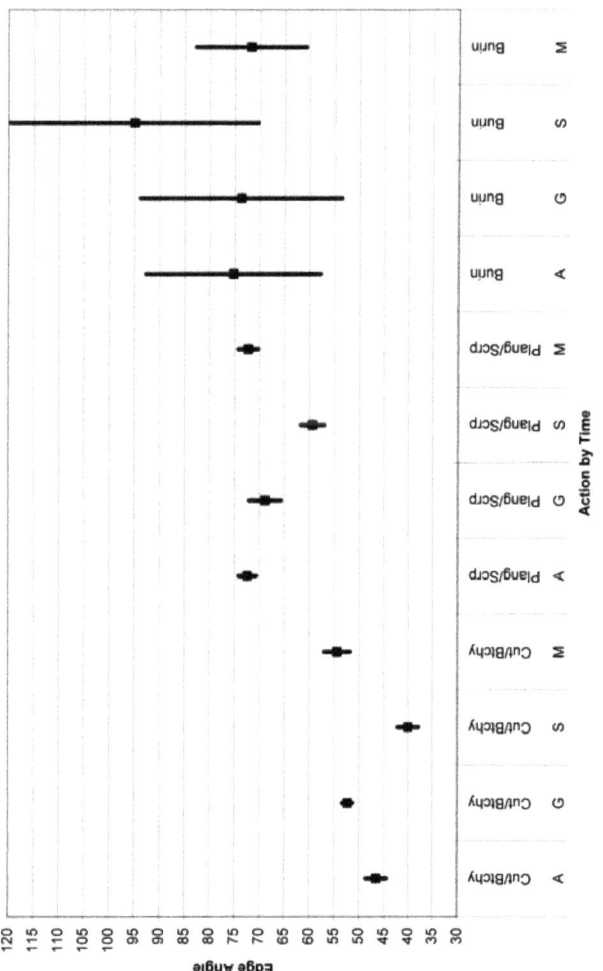

Figure 22: Edge angle ANOVA by use action and time period.

While these averages are lower than those seen in the hafted samples, they still fall within the lower range of the variability plotted for hafted tools for each time period. Each of the hand held samples is significantly different from the others.

Width/Thickness Ratios

To compare the degree of standardization between the time periods, the ratio of width to thickness measurements is calculated for the principal tools in the use-wear sample, and the resulting variance is analyzed using the GT2 method. Unretouched blades and flakes, burin spalls, and crested blades are excluded from the ANOVA calculations. The thought behind this comparison of ratios is that it has been argued earlier that more curated assemblages should show a higher degree of standardization with respect to tool dimension. The width and thickness measurements are chosen for this comparison so that all tools can be included in the comparisons. If length and width measurements are used for the ratio, only complete tools can be considered. The fragmentary nature of the use-wear samples means that few tools could be considered within each temporal sample, and the resulting patterns would be suspect.

There is a wide range of technological and metric variability between the time periods due to changes in tool forms and dimensions throughout the Upper Paleolithic. To normalize the calculated width to thickness ratios, the natural log (ln) of each ratio is calculated and these normalized values are used in the ANOVA calculation.

The calculated upper and lower comparison limits for the sample means of each cultural time period are graphed in Figure 28. The use-wear assemblages are not significantly different from one another; the null hypothesis is accepted. All of the samples have a similar range of variability between the calculated upper and lower limits.

The natural log normalized width/thickness ratios are also temporally compared for hafted and hand-held tools, and the ANOVA upper and lower comparison limits for the sample means are depicted in Figures 29 and 30, respectively. All sample means for the hafted tools exhibit a high amount of variability and all of the temporal samples are statistically the same, so the null hypothesis of no difference cannot be rejected. The Aurignacian sample is not included in this comparison because only one tool showed clear evidence of being hafted. A similar situation is true for the hand-held tools. While the range of variability is smaller for each temporal category, the null hypothesis is accepted since all of the calculated ranges overlap. Thus, no time period has hafted or hand-held tools that are more metrically standardized than the other time periods.

In another comparison of the width/thickness ratio (non-normalized data), a coefficient of variation (CV) is calculated for each temporal sample (Table 6). A coefficient of variation is a sample's standard deviation expressed as a percentage of the sample mean and is useful for comparing samples when they differ appreciably in their means (Sokal and Rohlf 1995:58). A lower value (percentage) means that there is less variability around the mean and therefore represents a more standardized toolkit (Shott 1986:43), which is indicative of curation. The sample that displays the least amount of variability is the Solutrean. The Aurignacian and Magdalenian calculations are essentially the same and higher than the Solutrean result. The highest amount of variability is seen in the Gravettian sample, which means that it has the lowest degree of standardization with respect to this normalized ratio. This is in contrast to the EU analysis, discussed below, which shows that the Gravettian sample is more versatile, and thus more curated.

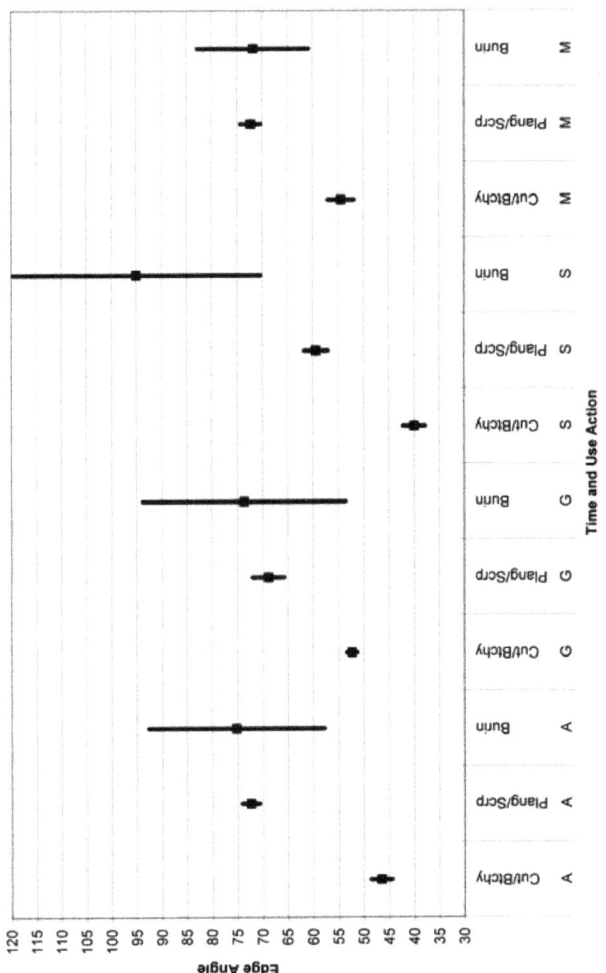

Figure 23: Edge angle ANOVA by time period and use action.

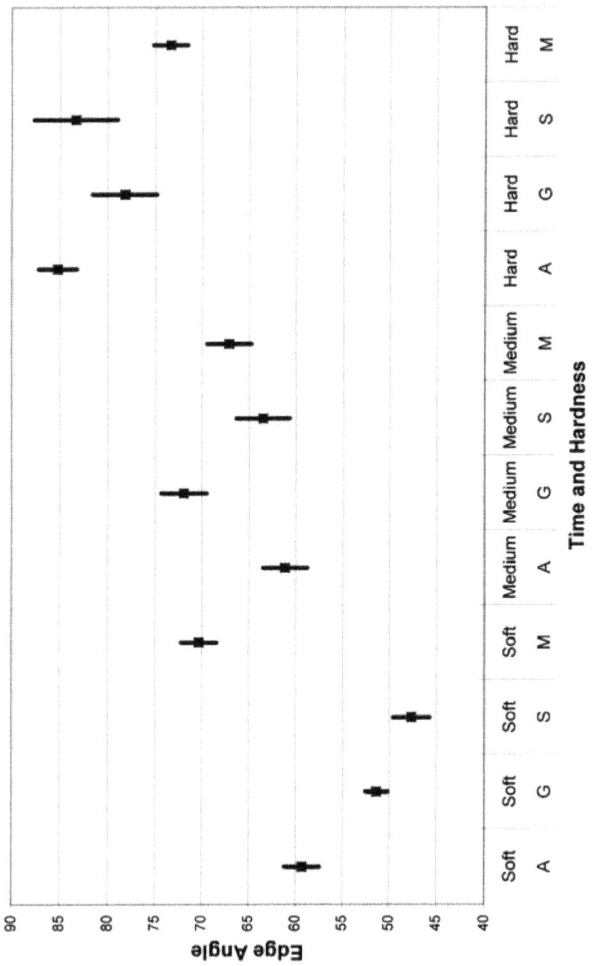

Figure 24: Edge angle ANOVA by hardness and time period.

Employable Unit Averages

Another comparison aimed at evaluating the degree of curation is the average number of employable units (EUs) per tool. It is assumed that tools in a curated toolkit will have a higher average number of EUs per tool than would be observed in an expedient, or more disposable, toolkit since curated tools must be more versatile (Shott 1986:35). The reason for this is that curated tools are used and maintained over a long period of time, therefore they have a higher likelihood of having more of their edges used over their life span. Expedient tools, on the other hand, are chosen to perform an immediate task at hand, and once that task is completed, they are typically discarded. They have a much lower probability of being used to complete multiple tasks or of being used over a long time span in comparison to curated tools. Because the sample sizes vary between the toolkit samples, the EU averages are standardized for comparative purposes. As was done with the ln normalized width/thickness ratios, a coefficient of variation is calculated for the EU averages and used to compare the assemblages. Samples with low CVs are

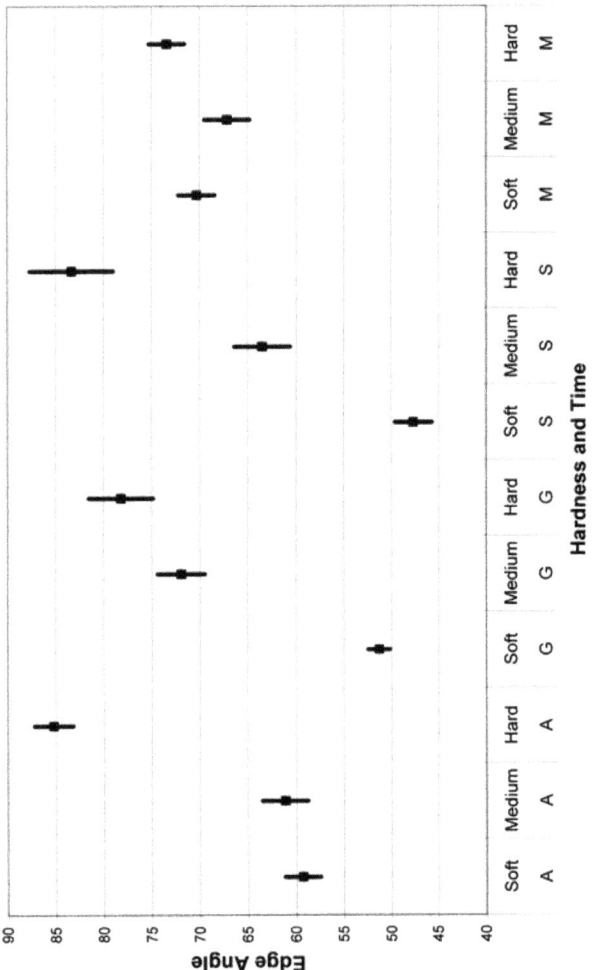

Figure 25: Edge angle ANOVA by time period and hardness.

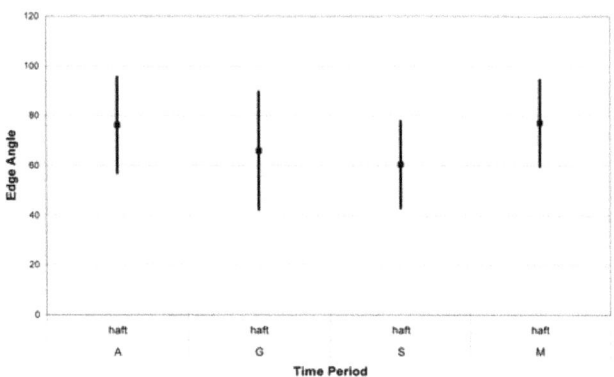

Figure 26: Edge angle ANOVA of hafted tools.

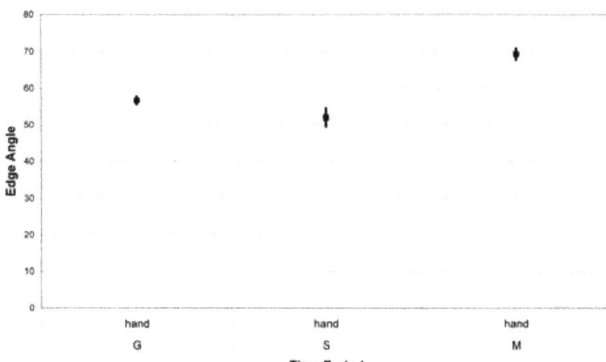

Figure 27: Edge angle ANOVA of hand-held tools.

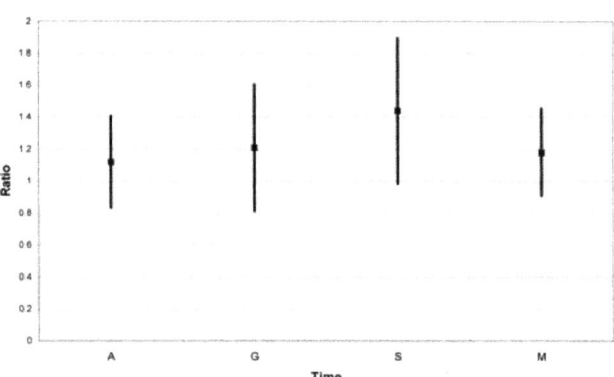

Figure 28: Natural log normalized width/thickness ratio ANOVA graph.

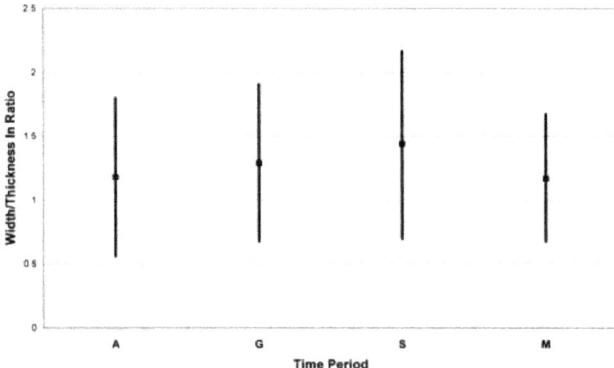

Figure 29: Natural log normalized width/thickness ratio ANOVA for hafted tools.

Table 6: Log normalized width/thickness ratio coefficient of variation.

Time Period	N	Mean	S.D.	CV
Aurignacian	23	3.30	1.35	40.91
Gravettian	12	3.63	1.80	49.59
Solutrean	9	4.40	1.27	28.86
Magdalenian	25	3.84	1.59	41.41

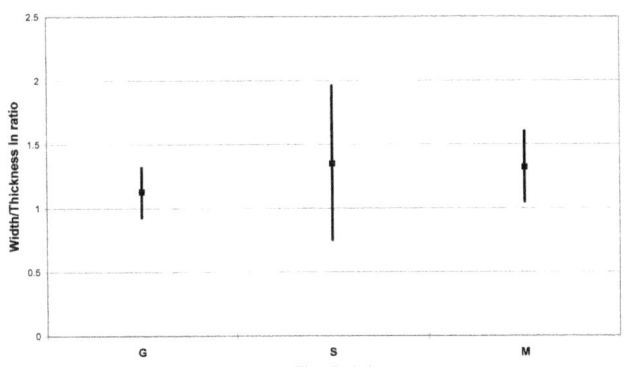

Figure 30: Natural log normalized width/thickness ANOVA for hand-held tools.

Table 7: Employable units' coefficient of variation.

Time Period	N	Mean	S.D.	CV
Aurignacian	40	1.2	0.687	57.25
Gravettian	44	1.36	0.613	45.07
Solutrean	25	1.52	0.714	46.97
Magdalenian	55	0.95	0.591	62.21

more versatile than those with high CVs (Shott 1986:43). The samples' employable unit CVs are contained in Table 7.

The Aurignacian sample has the second highest EU coefficient of variation (57.25) indicating that it has a low versatility score and thus can be considered less curated than those with lower CV scores. This result is unexpected since it goes counter to the chi-square results that indicated that its high frequency of hafted tools was a principal contributor to that significant chi-square result. I am reluctant to put more weight on the chi-square results than the EU CV calculation because the Aurignacian hafting sample is small (n = 8). The Gravettian and Solutrean samples have the lowest coefficients of variation and are essentially identical. These lower values indicate that these samples are more versatile than the Aurignacian and Magdalenian samples. The higher versatility represents a higher average number of use applications per tool, which I have argued is indicative of a curated toolkit.

The Solutrean sample has the highest average number of EUs per tool, and this is reflected in its low EU coefficient of variation. This indicates a more versatile and curated toolkit. This is not surprising considering the unique nature of Solutrean assemblages compared to the other blade dominated Upper Paleolithic cultures. The Solutrean is most well known for its bifacial tools, which are not present in other Western European Upper Paleolithic assemblages. While the two are not culturally related, the Solutrean shares many technological and material characteristics with the Clovis culture of the North America. Clovis assemblages of the Central Plains are highly curated and were used by mobile populations. It is not surprising that the Solutrean bifacial assemblage that dates to the Last Glacial Maximum has a characteristic that identifies it as being highly curated. A number of fragmentary bifacial tools were recovered from the I11, P16, and J10 excavation blocks and most of them have wear traces that indicate they were used as both projectiles and cutting tools (Figures 31 and 32). This pattern is commonly seen in early Paleoindian bifaces (Kay 1996, 1997, 1998, 2000). This type of tool use further substantiates the finding that these toolkits were highly curated.

The low CV value associated with the Gravettian assemblage was not expected since it is dominated by blades, is formal tool poor, and is dominated by butchery wear. However, the recovered lithic assemblages indicate that little lithic reduction took place on site during the Gravettian time period. It seems that Gravettian groups were arriving at Solutré with a prefabricated toolkit dominated by blades. Therefore, despite a narrow range of activities and a blade dominated toolkit, which initially are assumed to indicate an expedient toolkit, it appears that Gravettian groups were conducting activities at the site with a limited but curated toolkit.

The Magdalenian sample has the highest EU coefficient of variation indicating that it is less versatile and thus less curated (Shott 1986:43). This assemblage has a high percentage of hafted tools, which is assumed to be characteristics of a curated toolkit, thus contradicting the EU CV result. One explanation for this pattern is that the Magdalenian assemblage recovered from Solutré is composed of very specialized and hafted tools. While hafting is assumed to be a proxy measure of curation, it is possible that many of these specialized tools had to be hafted to be optimally functional. The need for hafting would result in a higher signature of standardization. Therefore, the high frequency of hafting likely is not indicative of high mobility and curation, but rather functional specialization. Additionally, the bulk of the Magdalenian use-wear sample comes from block P16. The lithic assemblage recovered from this excavation block had exhausted cores and core platform rejuvenation flakes, indicating that tools were being manufactured on site. Since these specialized tools needed to be hafted in order to be efficient, I propose that they were produced on site, placed in hafting elements brought to the site, and once they were exhausted or the task was completed, they possibly were discarded on site and replaced with new tools in anticipation of future activities away from Solutré.

TYPOLOGY

I stated earlier that one goal of this analysis was to evaluate the correspondence between tool function and typology. Some studies that have concluded that tool function is not closely related to tool type were described. This is not the case with the Solutré use-wear samples. With the exception of a few individual tools, the Solutré samples from each cultural component show a close relationship between

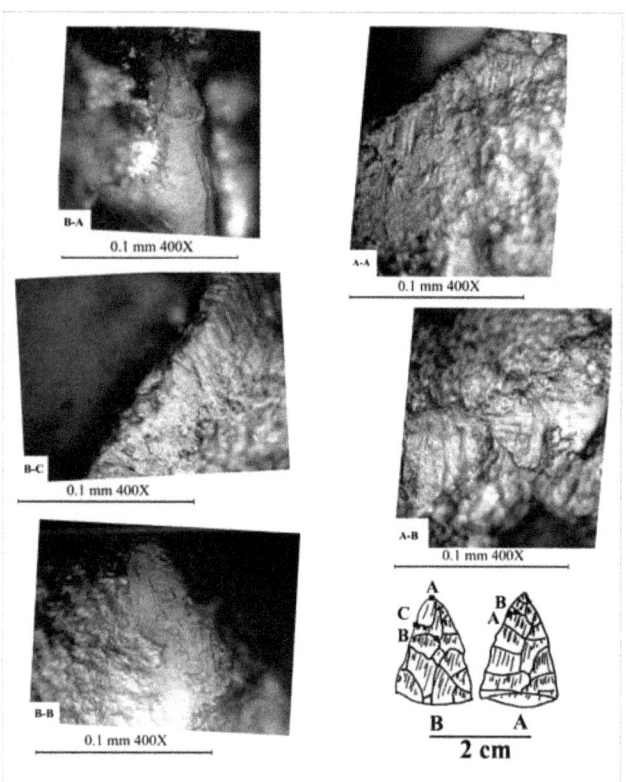

Figure 31: I11u88-1708 – Solutrean example of impact and butchery.

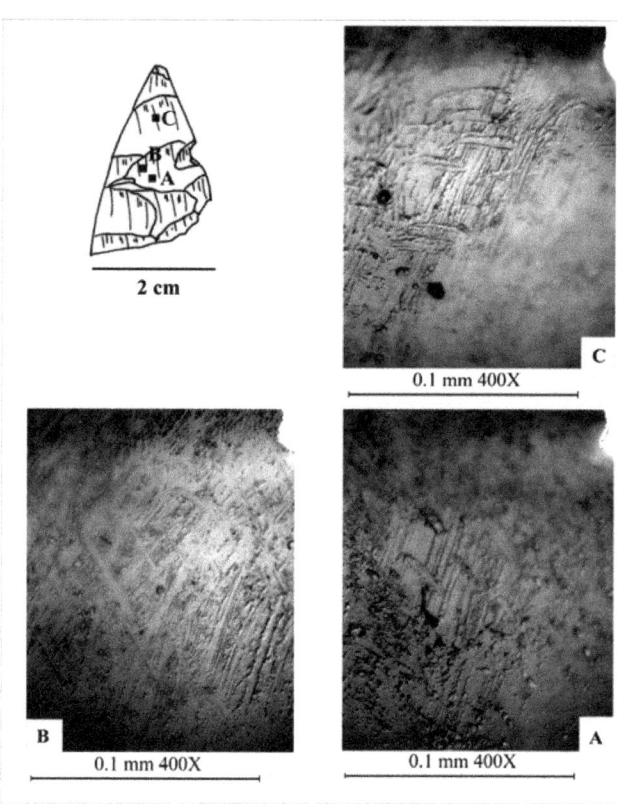

Figure 32: J10u27-1 – Solutrean example of impact and butchery.

tool function and typology. In other words, blades predominantly were used to cut, scrapers were used to scrape, burins were used to groove, etc. When one looks at the database, one does see some variability in the correspondence between typology and worked material, though. For instance, it is typically assumed that scrapers are used to process hides, and due to fact that large numbers of animals were killed and butchered at Solutré, one would expect to see such a pattern at Solutré throughout the Upper Paleolithic. While this is essentially the case, the Aurignacian sample is an exception to this expectation because the scrapers show a high frequency of use on hard and medium contact materials such as wood, bone, and antler. I have argued previously (Banks 2002a) that this indicates retooling of the non-lithic components of the toolkit after the kill events and in anticipation of future use.

Related to typology and corresponding tool morphology, Figures 22 and 24 show that low edge angles correspond to cutting activities, medium range edge angles correspond to scraping activities, and higher edge angles are associated with burin and grooving actions. The wide range of edge angle variability and burin use is likely due to the presence of broken tools used as ad hoc burins. A similar pattern holds true for edge angle correspondence with worked material hardness. Figure 24 shows a clear relationship between increasing edge angles and harder contact materials.

CHAPTER 8: SUMMARY AND CONCLUSIONS

The previous chapters have described the methodology and results of the use-wear analyses of lithic samples from the different Upper Paleolithic cultural components at Solutré, and the results are briefly summarized below.

The resolution of the archaeological components, or the degree to which they have undergone post-depositional modification, has been described in earlier chapters. The Gravettian, characterized by the consolidated sediments and cultural materials termed the "magma", exhibits the highest degree of disturbance and likely is in a completely secondary context. A similar case holds true for the Magdalenian materials encountered in sector I11. The upper Aurignacian levels appear to have been deposited on a level surface and suffered little disturbance, but the faunal long bone elements in the lower Aurignacian levels have a strong directional orientation and are likely in a disturbed context. On the other hand, the Solutrean component documented in sector I11 is level, is interpreted to represent an activity area around a hearth, and appears to be relatively undisturbed. The Solutrean artifacts recovered from P16 may be in place, but it is possible that they originated in contexts upslope from P16 and moved downslope prior to Magdalenian occupations. As has been discussed previously, there is some debate as to the resolution of the Magdalenian record of block P16. I have pointed out earlier that Combier (2002b) concludes that P16 represents an intact, or at least partially intact, activity area, and Montet-White (2002b) proposes that the spatial organization of certain tool classes reflect intact post-kill processing activity areas. Turner (2002), however, concludes that the majority of cultural materials recovered from P16 are in an ancient erosional gully. Therefore, natural site formation processes have differentially influenced the cultural materials recovered from each area recently excavated at Solutré, and most are either highly disturbed or partially disturbed. This makes temporal comparisons of discrete site events and activity spatial organization impossible. Based on the disturbed nature of the cultural components, the fact that each cultural component likely represents multiple events that occurred over a long period of time, and the need to lump the lithic use-wear samples into broad temporal categories, one must keep in mind that the patterns discussed below are general in nature. It is almost certain that during each time period there was some variability in the strategies of site use, but over large spans of time certain trends do emerge. Despite site formation factors, this use-wear analysis has demonstrated that inter-cultural differences in site use can be observed, and that functional contrasts between the components are discernable. The findings summarized below reflect the dominant or average pattern associated with each cultural complex.

The Aurignacian sample has a high frequency of scraping and planing activities on medium and hard contact materials, and a relatively low occurrence of butchery and cutting on softer contact materials. While the sample of tools that exhibit hafting and prehension wear traces is small, it is likely representative since this time period is relatively lithic poor at Solutré. Relative to the sample, there is a high frequency of tools with hafting use-wear signatures. With respect to edge rounding, the Aurignacian has numerous tools with only minor edge rounding and a low frequency of moderate edge rounding. While it is clear that animals were being killed and processed in the area of the site designated as M12, this sample indicates that other activities were taking place.

Combier and White (2002b) conclude that Aurignacian groups occupied Solutré for brief periods of time and arrived on site with prepared toolkits geared towards hunting and processing. The use-wear data seemingly contradict this hypothesis. The use-wear data indicate that Aurignacian groups were likely residentially mobile within the region immediately surrounding Solutré, and were typically arriving at Solutré in anticipation of the horse herds migrating through the landscape immediately southeast of the site. This pattern of arriving on site prior to the animals and gearing up before herd interception is similar to the behavior seen during the Magdalenian period at Verberie (Enloe 2000a, 2000b). It is likely that subsequent to their arrival Aurignacian groups prepared the hunting and processing components of their toolkit prior to the arrival of migratory game. The presence of crested blades, core platform rejuvenation flakes, and hearth features all support such a finding. It is also possible that these use-wear and lithic reduction signatures represent such activities taking place subsequent to kill events, but I think this is less likely. While many of the Aurignacian tools were hafted, thus indicating curation and possible logistic mobility, a majority of the tools exhibit polishes that exhibit only minor or moderate rounding over employed edges. Such a pattern is not expected for a versatile, extensively-used, and curated toolkit employed by highly residentially mobile groups or logistically mobile teams. The Aurignacian groups that frequented Solutré were probably residentially mobile (which accounts for the relatively high frequency of hafted tools), were restricted in their movements to the immediate region and had ready access to lithic raw materials, arrived at the site prior to the arrival of game animals and tooled up on site prior to kill activities. Because Aurignacian toolkits contain bone, and sometimes antler, armatures, and many hafting elements were likely made of bone or antler, the high frequency of hard contact material wear traces supports this hypothesis.

The Gravettian sample is markedly different. This assemblage is dominated by unretouched and retouched blades used in butchery and kill activities, and while the patterns are not significant, many of these butchery tools have polishes that are moderately to well rounded over tool edges. In addition, the EU coefficients of variation indicate that the Gravettian toolkits were highly versatile and thus curated. The use-wear results show a significantly high frequency of butchery and cutting wear, a significantly low frequency of scraping and planing activities, and a low occurrence of working hard contact materials. This sample is also marked by a high number of hand-held tools and few hafted tools. Finally, it is associated with a high edge angle average for these animal processing activities. A large number of these tools are retouched, and such a pattern would be typical if groups arrived on site with a narrow range of anticipated activities and a restricted toolkit composed of tools needing frequent rejuvenation since they could not be easily replaced with new tools. These data indicate that Gravettian groups were logistically mobile, resided in the region around Solutré, and arrived on site with toolkits that were geared towards the killing and processing of game animals. They arrived on site with a pre-made toolkit that was used intensively over a short period of time. While tool stone was available within a radius of several kilometers, time was likely not available to travel and obtain stone for refurbishing their existing toolkits. So, the conclusions of Combier (2002d) are supported by the use-wear data, meaning that the Gravettian groups operated within a relatively restricted region. The use-wear data indicate that small, logistically organized, special purpose groups used Solutré during this time period. These data support the conclusions of Combier and Montet-White (2002b) concerning the Gravettian occupations of Solutré.

The Solutrean sample is markedly different from the previous Upper Paleolithic samples. There is no significant variation with respect to expected tool actions. Also, there is low frequency of hard contact material processing. The sample has a high curation signature, a wide range of tool types present, and the relative abundance of retouched tools, especially the bifacially retouched pieces, indicates a curated assemblage. The EU coefficient of variation calculations show this sample to be highly curated, which is not surprising considering its similarity to early North American Paleoindian assemblages. I would argue that these groups are highly mobile and that their mobility could be classified as residential. They most likely exploited a wider territory than Gravettain populations and incorporated Solutré into it when the season and opportunity was right. The presence of laurel leaf projectile points made from crystal support this conclusion since such raw materials are exotic. The significantly low edge angles associated with tools used in cutting and scraping activities indicate that Solutrean groups used Solutré soon after they had produced new tools and refurbished their toolkits. Solutrean groups likely arrived in the Mâconnais region prior to the arrival of migratory game animals, refurbished their toolkits, and then moved to Solutré to procure and process game. The use-wear data support the conclusions of Combier and Montet-White (2002b) who propose that Solutrean groups were highly mobile and likely occupied Solutré for longer periods of time than groups did in earlier time periods.

The Magdalenian sample is different from the others. It is characterized by a diverse toolkit and has a low curation signature. It does, though, have a high frequency of hafted tools, which would seemingly contradict the low curation signature. In addition, this sample shows a high average edge angle for cutting activities, a pattern seemingly typical of versatile and curated toolkits. This cultural component's sample has a low frequency of butchery wear and work on soft contact materials. It is also represented by a high frequency of burin actions and contact with hard contact materials, a pattern that would at first seem to indicate on-site camp activities or activities not associated with the processing of dispatched game. These patterns seem at first difficult to sort out. It is possible that they indicate that Magdalenian populations were residentially mobile and covered a wide area in their seasonal movements, a pattern proposed by Combier and Montet-White (2002b). Another explanation, though, is that Magdalenian groups were logistically organized and had base camps nearby. While they may have used a large region that included areas around and to the west of Mâcon, as well as uplands in the Jura Mountains to the east, special purpose groups may have intensively exploited Solutré during brief visits while the larger population occupied seasonal base camps nearby. Such an interpretation is supported by the fact that the Magdalenian lithic assemblages indicate that prepared cores were brought to the site; possibly to produce tools probably needed to replace exhausted ones. These new tools were likely carried away from the site. Magdalenian tools appear to be highly specialized, and it is likely that this specialization required they be hafted. Thus, the curation signature related to hafting and the high frequency of work on medium and hard contact materials is likely the result of creating, hafting, and using specialized tools and not related to curation or residential mobility requiring a curated toolkit. While my interpretation is possible, the use-wear data do not clearly contradict the conclusions of Combier and Montet-White (2002b) concerning Magdalenian use of the site.

In Chapter 5, different findings related to typology and tool function were reviewed. In some studies, the conclusions have been that typology and function are not closely correlated, but such findings have been contradicted in use-wear analyses of other site assemblages. The Solutré use-wear data show a close correlation between typology and tool function throughout the Upper Paleolithic. This may be the result of the consistency in principal site use over such a long period of time, but it also may indicate that typology and function were closely correlated during the Upper Paleolithic. This would suggest that the methods of examination in the studies that show great variability in the type/function relationship may be suspect, or that those assemblages may represent exceptions to the rule.

The high degree of post-depositional modification of Solutré's cultural components, the long spans of time represented by each cultural component, and the subsequent need to lump artifacts into broad temporal categories all made the attempt to address stone tool use and site activities at Solutré challenging. Nonetheless, the use-wear methods and analysis of the recorded use-wear attributes allowed for the identification of temporal differences in secondary site activities. The findings of tool use and toolkit versatility allow the current conclusions of site activities and site exploitation to be tested, refined, or labeled as in need of further investigation, and demonstrate the usefulness of high-power use-wear methods towards understanding human tool use by allowing researchers to indirectly see a tool's ancient behavioral context.

Finally, this study has demonstrated the utility of high-power use-wear methodologies when attempting to complete a chaîne opératoire. The methods used in this analysis have allowed us to see how tools were used, how intensively they were used, the degree to which they were resharpened, and at what point in their use cycle they were discarded (or lost). Such clarity is not always possible with analyses that rely solely on typological and technological conclusions based on form and metrics. All of the previous studies on the Solutré assemblages have been performed from a standpoint of type and technology, while function and use have only been assumed and never confirmed. This functional analysis has supported some conclusions from the previous analyses, but it has also contradicted and challenged other conclusions. It is hoped that this analysis has shown how powerful high-power use-wear methods can be when attempting to answer questions related to stone tool technology and site use, and how critical such methods are for taking a chaîne opératoire to its intended conclusion.

Appendix A: Experimental Tool List

Tool 1 - secondary flake (25% cortex) with distal hinge fracture used for skin removal by Hofman. Started at 11:55 and ran to 12:50. Noted small fractures and dulling at 12:25.

Tool 2 - complete backed blade used by Will Banks for skinning. Times of use are 12:05-12:20, 12:33-12:35, 12:37-12:41, 12:43-12:50. Dulling noticed at 12:25 but no visible edge damage.

Tool 3 - naturally backed blade - distal fragment - used by Hofman to eviscerate deer. 1:32-1:44.

Tool 4 - early stage blade - cortex on one edge - used by Hofman for dismemberment and meat separation on the hind quarters. Also used to separate the thorax from the neck. Meat removal from thorax (removal of sirloin). 1:46-1:50 and 1:51-2:26.

Tool 5 - early stage blade - very robust - used by Will Banks to: remove forelimbs, metapoidal removals from both fore and hindlimbs, meat removal from hind limb, and femur/tibia separation. 2:02-2:04 and 2:05-2:17. Tool noted as very dull at 2:10.

Tool 6 - flake used by Will to separate the femur and tibia, hitting bone occasionally. Tool dulled very quickly. 2:22-2:26.

Tool 7 - blade - natural cortex backing - hinge termination. Used by Will for meat removal from the hind limb (occasionally hitting bone), meat removal from the forelimb and neck. 2:28-3:00.

Tool 8 - tertiary flake/blade - no cortex. Used to fillet rib cage and thoracic verts. Held by proximal end. Bone contact was occasional. The non-working edge was dulled with an abrader in mid-work. Also used to skin and clean the deer=s skull. 2:29-3:00.

Tool 9 - flake with some cortex used by Virginia Hatfield to remove meat from forelimb and lumbar verts. Occasional bone contact. 2:43-3:18 and 3:18-3:26.

Tool 10 - tertiary flake used by Hofman to deflesh the innominate and cervical verts. 3:02-3:14 and 3:14 to 3:24 respectively.

Tool 11 - blade used to fillet meat.

Tool 12 - small flake used to remove meat and connective tissue from deer hide.

Tool 13 - blade used to cut and plane a green maple branch. Supple bark was removed. Sawing motion was back and forth with tool edge. Planing used same tool edge and tool was pulled toward the user.

Tool 14 - scraper used to scrape and plane green maple branch.

Tool 15 - tool used to cut frozen deer hide. Back and forth, and pulling cutting motion.

Tool 16 - tool used to cut fat and tissue from the interior of frozen and thawed deer hide.

Tool 17 - Cutting fat/meat from thawed deer hide.

Tool 18 - tool used to plane and scrape dry hard wood.

Tool 19 - unused tool, but edge was retouched with a deer antler billet to record types of wear produced by such retouch.

Tool 20 - grooving/cutting soaked antler. This tool is made from flint local to Solutré.

Tool 21 - grooving/scraping soaked antler.

Tool 22 - grooving soaked antler. This tool is made from flint local to Solutré.

Tool 23 - scraper used to scrape fresh/thawed deer hide - interior of hide.

Tool 24 (bis) - The bis would indicate that two tools have the number 24. This tool (photomicrographs labeled bis) was used to cut fresh deer hide and fatty tissue.

Tool 25 - tool used to scrape fresh deer hide - brief use.

Tool 26 – burin used to groove and initiate slotting on a soaked unweathered bison scapula. The grooving was done on each side of the dorsal spine to facilitate its removal. Raw material is Niobrara Jasper. Extensive use. Hand-held. Used until exhausted/non-functional.

Tool 27 – burin on break used to groove soaked and unweathered bison scapula for dorsal spine removal. Niobrara jasper, relatively brief use. Hand-held.

Tool 28 – retouched blade with natural backing – Niobrara jasper. Tool used to slot and cut an existing groove (made with tools 26 and 27) along the dorsal spine of a soaked and unweathered scapula. Extensive use. Retouched once during use to re-denticulate the edge. Hand-held. Used until exhausted/non-functional.

Tool 29 – denticulated blade/flake used to slot a groove on a soaked and unweathered bison scapula. Hand-held. Moderate to extensive use. Niobrara jasper.

Tool 30 – Burin on break (broken flake; Niobrara jasper). Juncture of retouch and break used as a burin to groove dry but unweathered bison scapula. Grooving was done on both sides of the dorsal spine to facilitate removal. Use was extensive – approximately 40 minutes. Hand-held.

Tool 41 - Edwards chert flake used to cut/saw green maple branch. Smaller twigs were removed. by sawing with serrated edge. The same edge was used to plane or scrape away bark and underlying tissue. Edge opposite serrated edge was used also for limited cutting and planing. Small distal projection was used in conjunction with non serrated edge to notch branch to produce a slot for hafting a lithic implement. Hand-held. Tool was used until the edge was no longer effective for cutting. An attempt was made to clean the edge with fingers, but edge was never resharpened. This heavy utilization with no rejuvenation and the cleaning strokes were an attempt to recreate patterns seen on the Solutré tools.

Tool 42 - Edwards chert flake with retouched lateral edge. Lateral edge was used to plane and scrape pine branch to produce foreshaft-like tool component. Both edges at distal end of tool were used for planing. Leading edges were used primarily in a pushing motion, although some back and forth motion did occur. Hand-held. Tool edge began to get noticeably duller.

Tool 43 - Double-ended burin made of Edwards chert. Both burin ends were used to groove soaked antler that had begun to dry somewhat. The burin bits deteriorated relatively quickly. One burin facet was used to plane the soaked antler in a back and forth motion. This facet is where the majority of the use-wear was located.

Tool 44 - small bladelet used by Tod Bevitt to field dress a deer. The initial observations were made of the tool without cleaning, so blood and tissue residues are visible in the photomicrographs. Field dressing consisted of opening the hide from chest to rectum, and cutting connective tissue in the gut.

Tool 45 - Blade used to cut pumpkin rind. Back and forth, along with pulling, cutting motion, and some wedging/splitting. Distal end was retouched and used to scrape out interior pumpkin flesh.

Tool 46 - Blade used by Luke Davis to butcher three wild birds (two duck, one Canada goose). Distal left corner, distal blade termination, and right lateral edge used to primarily remove breast meat. Hand held.

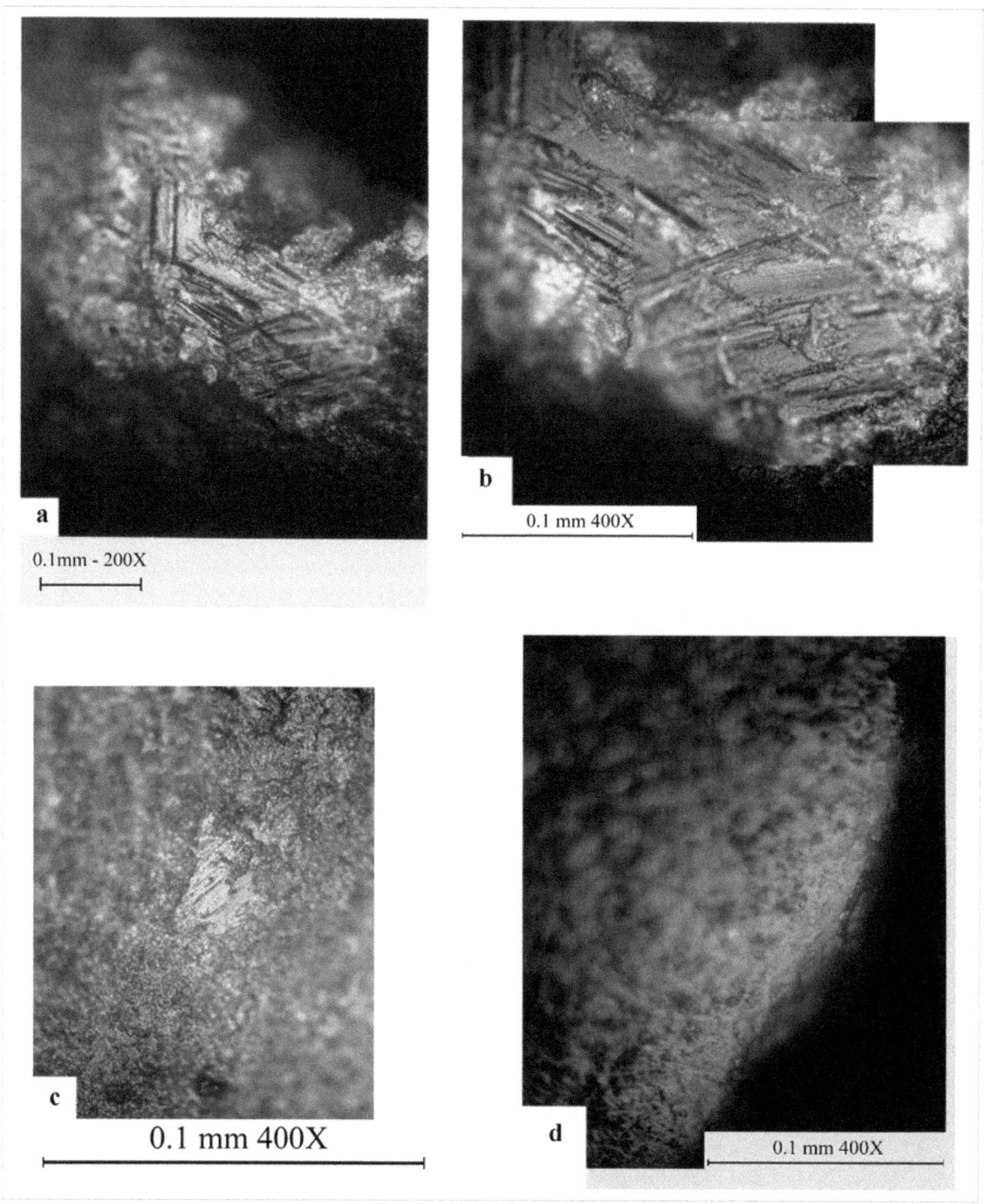

Appendix B-1: *a) WEB1A@200X – butchery; b) WEB1A@400X – butchery; c) WEB11A@400X – prehension; d) WEB18B@400X – planing dry hard wood.*

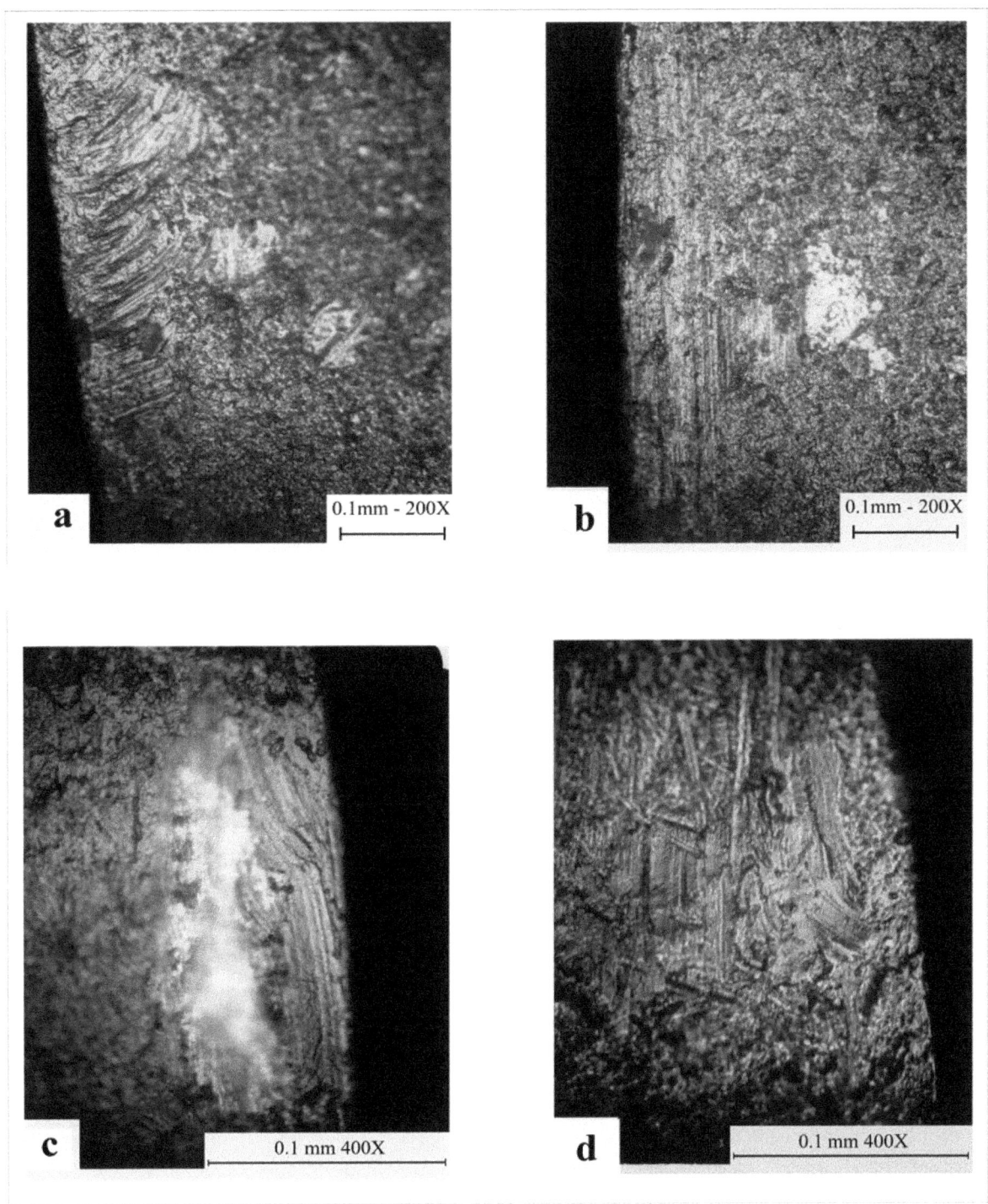

Appendix B-2: *a) WEB5A@200X – butchery; b) WEB5B@200X – butchery; c) WEB5C@400X – butchery; d) WEB5D@400X – butchery.*

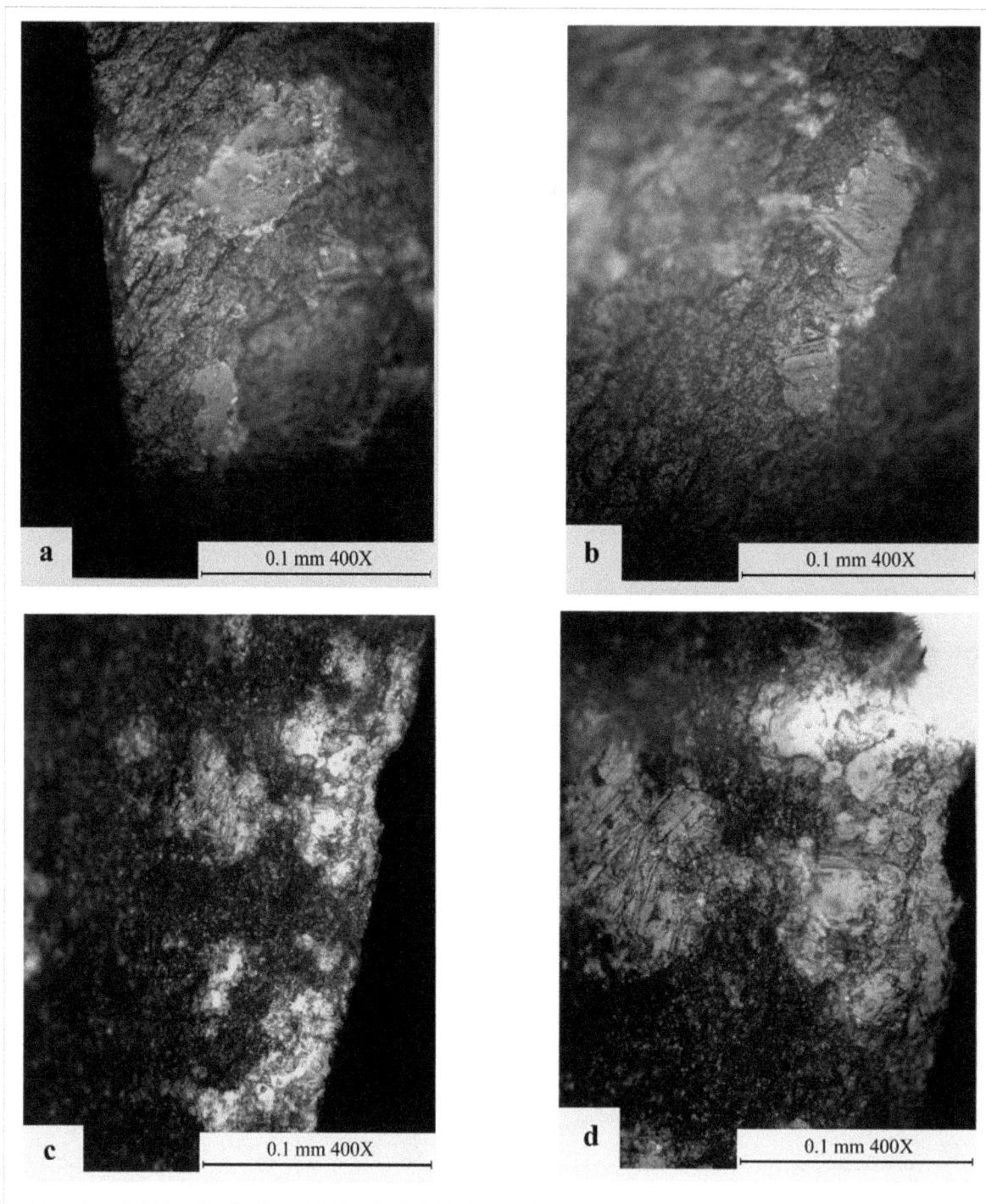

Appendix B-3: *a) WEB13A1@400X – wood work; b) WEB13A2@400X – wood work; c) WEB16A@100X (photo M. Kay) – cutting hide; d) WEB16A@200X (photo M. Kay) – cutting hide.*

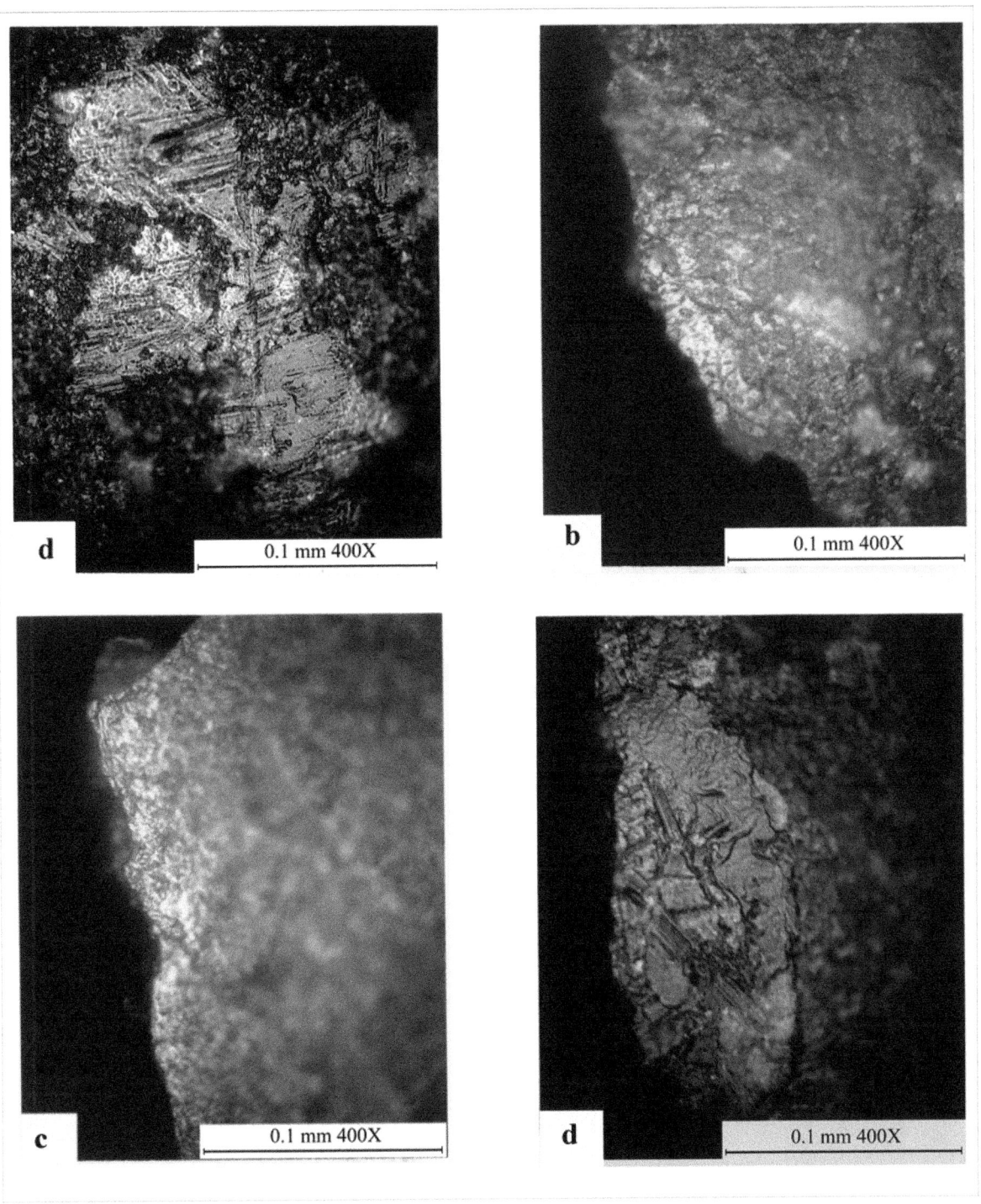

Appendix B-4: *a) WEB16A@400x – cutting hide; b) WEB 19A@400X (photo by M. Kay) – antler billet retouch; c) WEB 19B@400X (photo by M. Kay) – antler billet retouch; d) WEB19C@400X (photo by M. Kay) – antler billet retouch.*

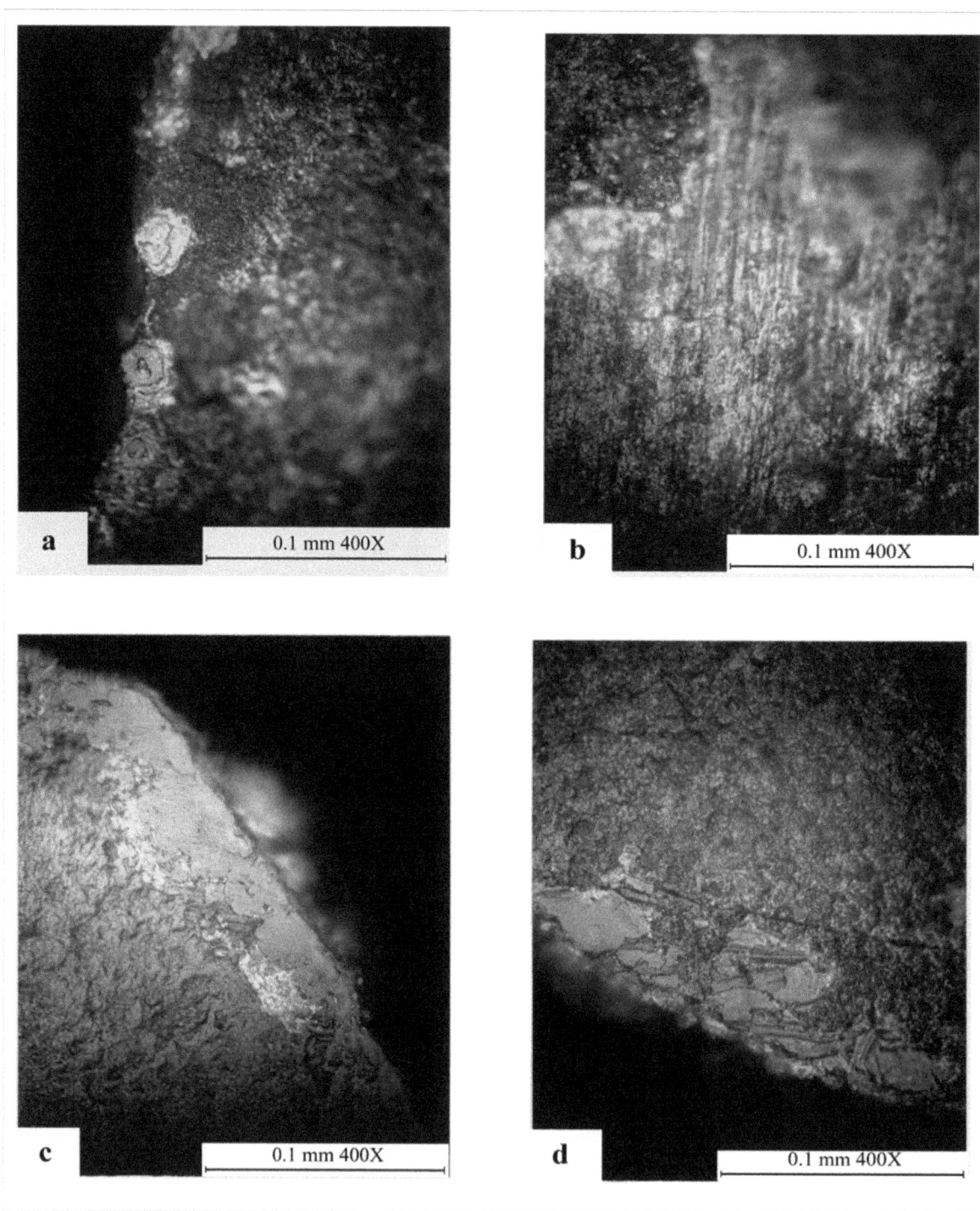

Appendix B-5*: Web19d@400X (photo by M. Kay) – antler billet retouch; b) WEB20A@400X – antler work; c) WEB21A@400X – antler work; d) WEB23A@400X – hide scraping.*

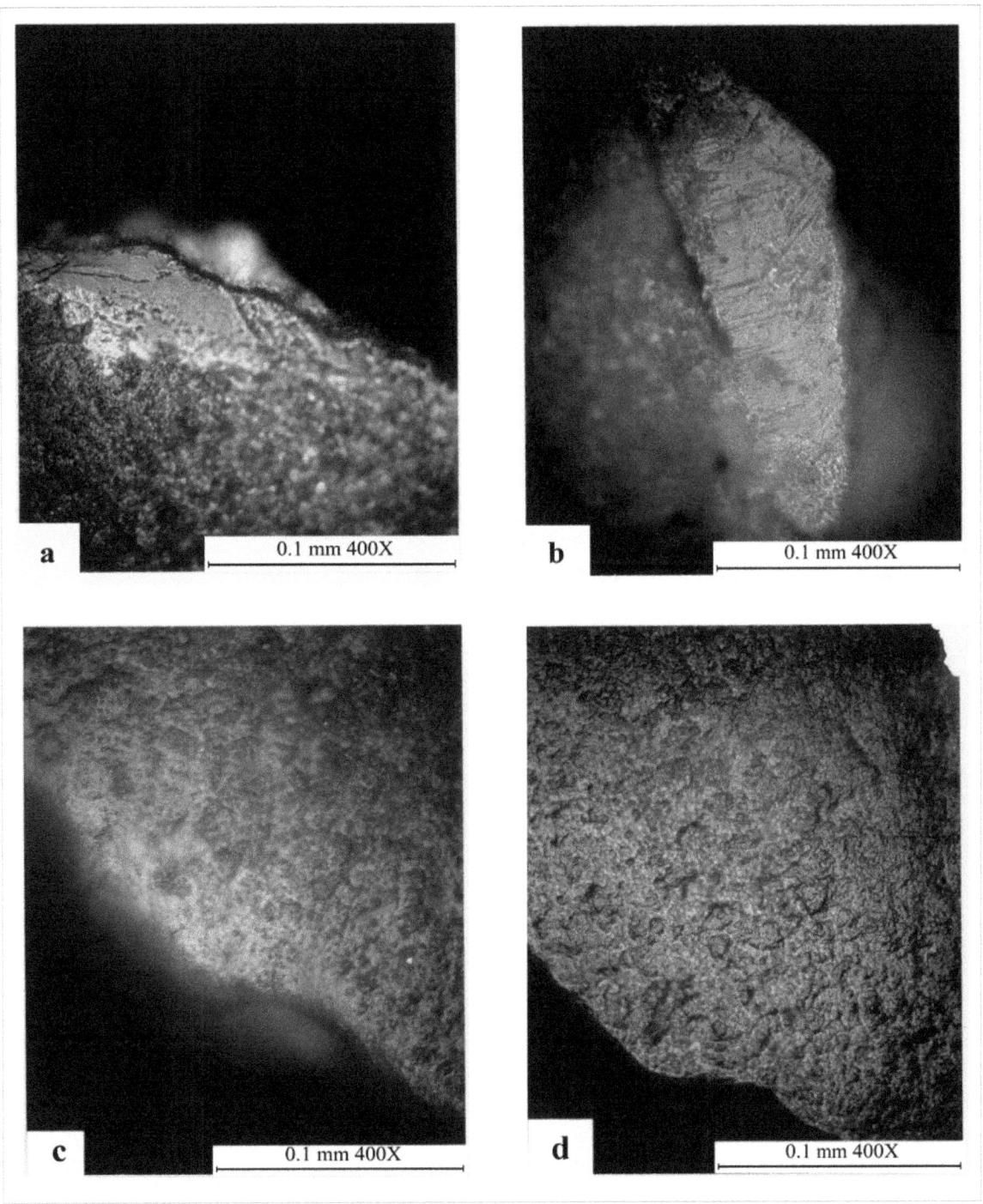

Appendix B-6*: a) WEB23B@400X – hide scraping; b) WEB23C@400X – hide scraping; c) WEB25A@400X – hide scraping; d) WEB25B@400X – hide scraping.*

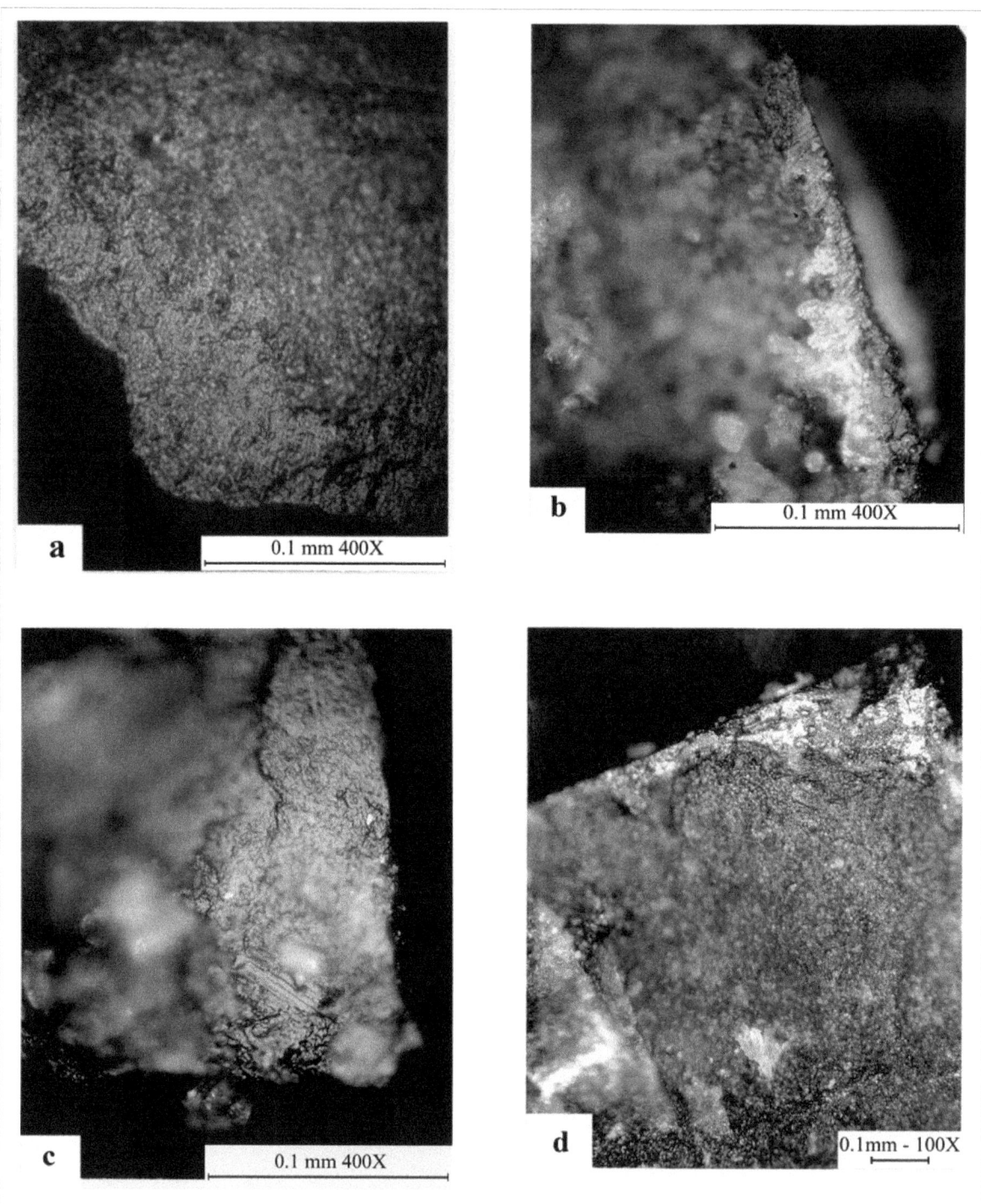

Appendix B-7*: WEB25C@400X – hide scraping; b) WEB26A@400X (photo by M. Kay) – burin on bone; c) WEB26B@400X (photo by M. Kay) – burin on bone; d) WEB27A@100X (photo by M. Kay) – burin on bone.*

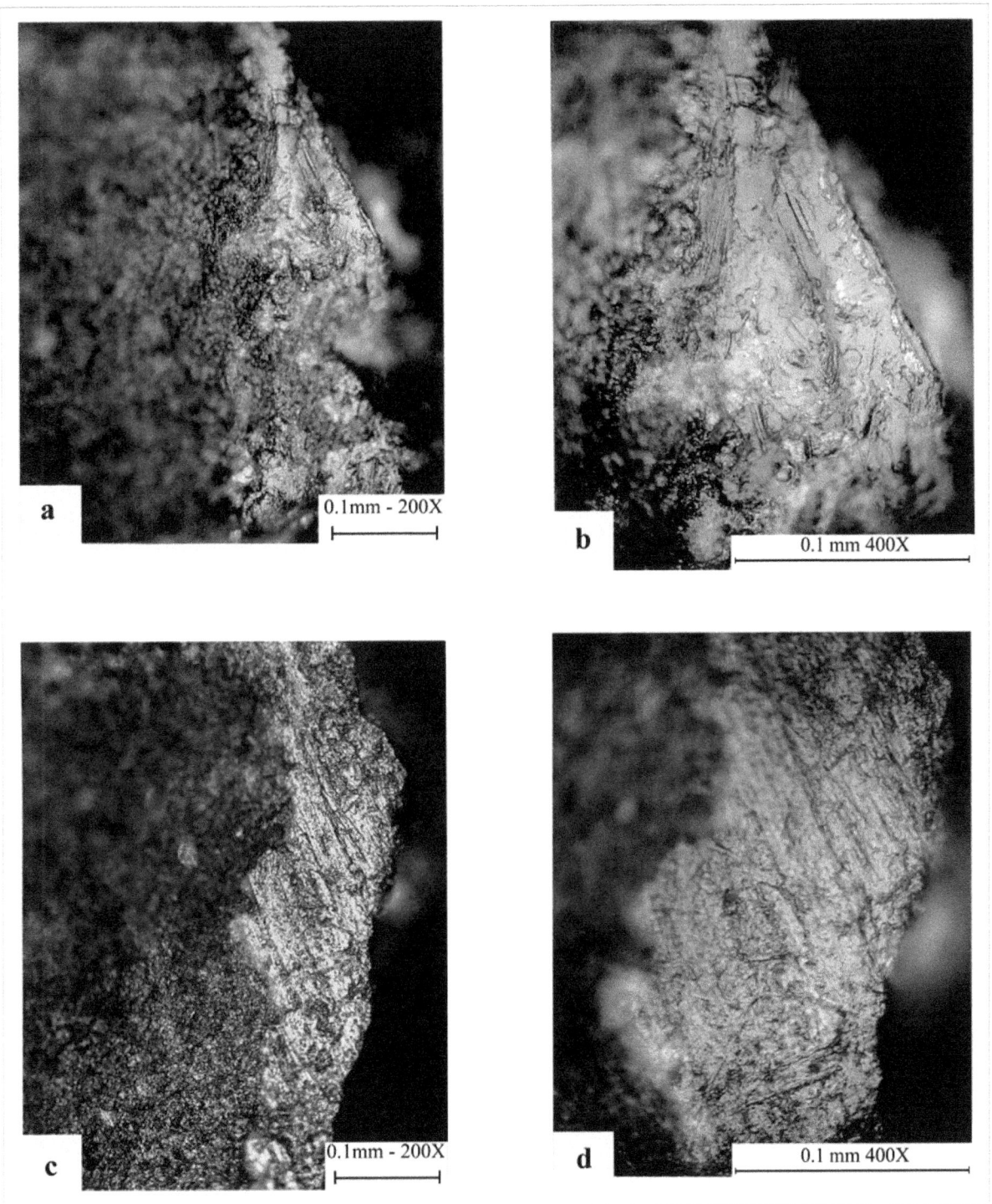

Appendix B-8: *a) WEB27A@200X (photo by M. Kay) – burin on bone; b) WEB27A@400X (photo by M. Kay) – burin on bone; c) WEB29A@200X (photo by M. Kay) – burin on bone; d) WEB29A@400X (photo by M. Kay) – burin on bone.*

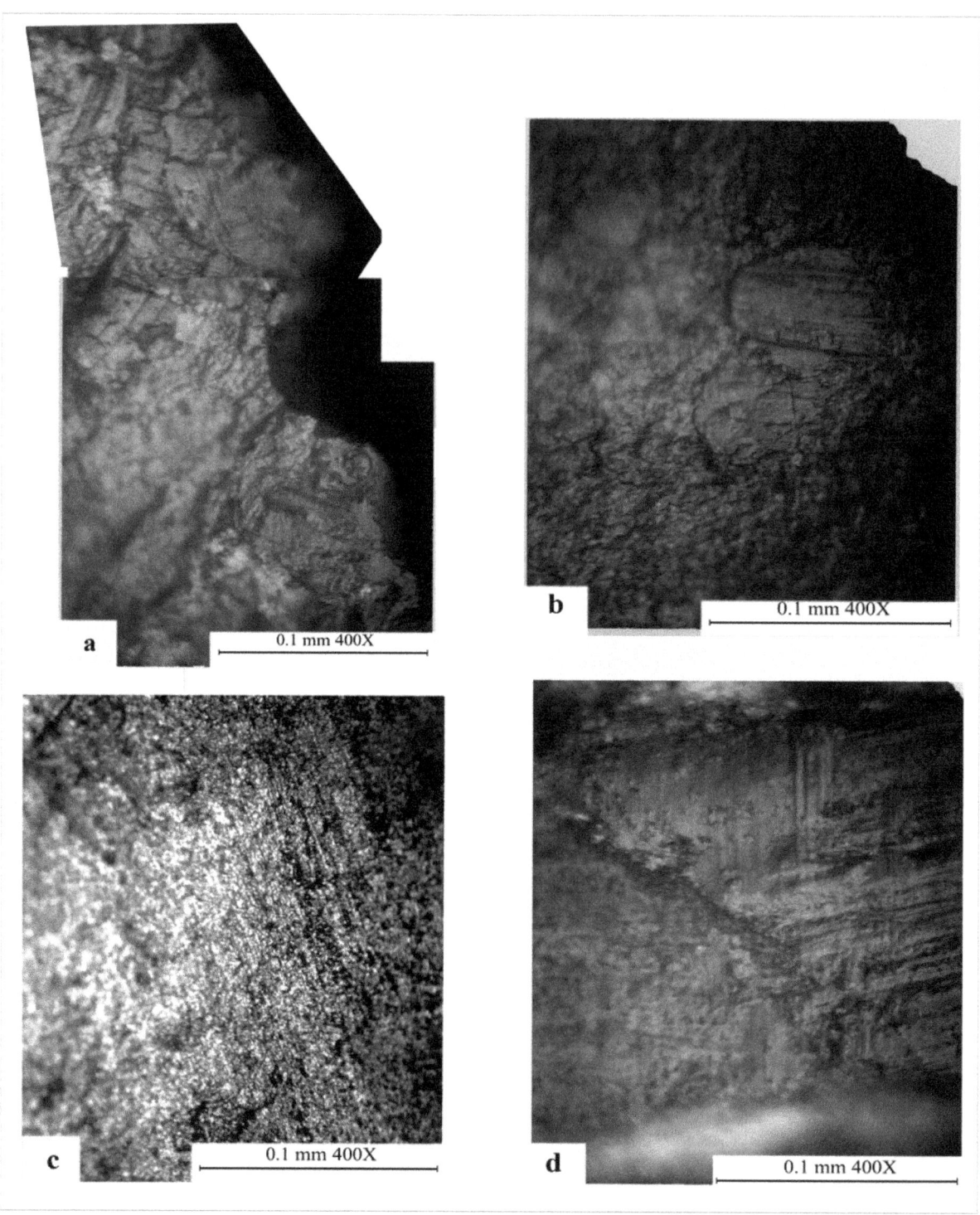

Appendix B-9*: a) WEB41A1/A2@400X – wood work; b) WEB41B@400X – wood work; c) WEB41D@400X – wood work; d) WEB43A@400X – antler work.*

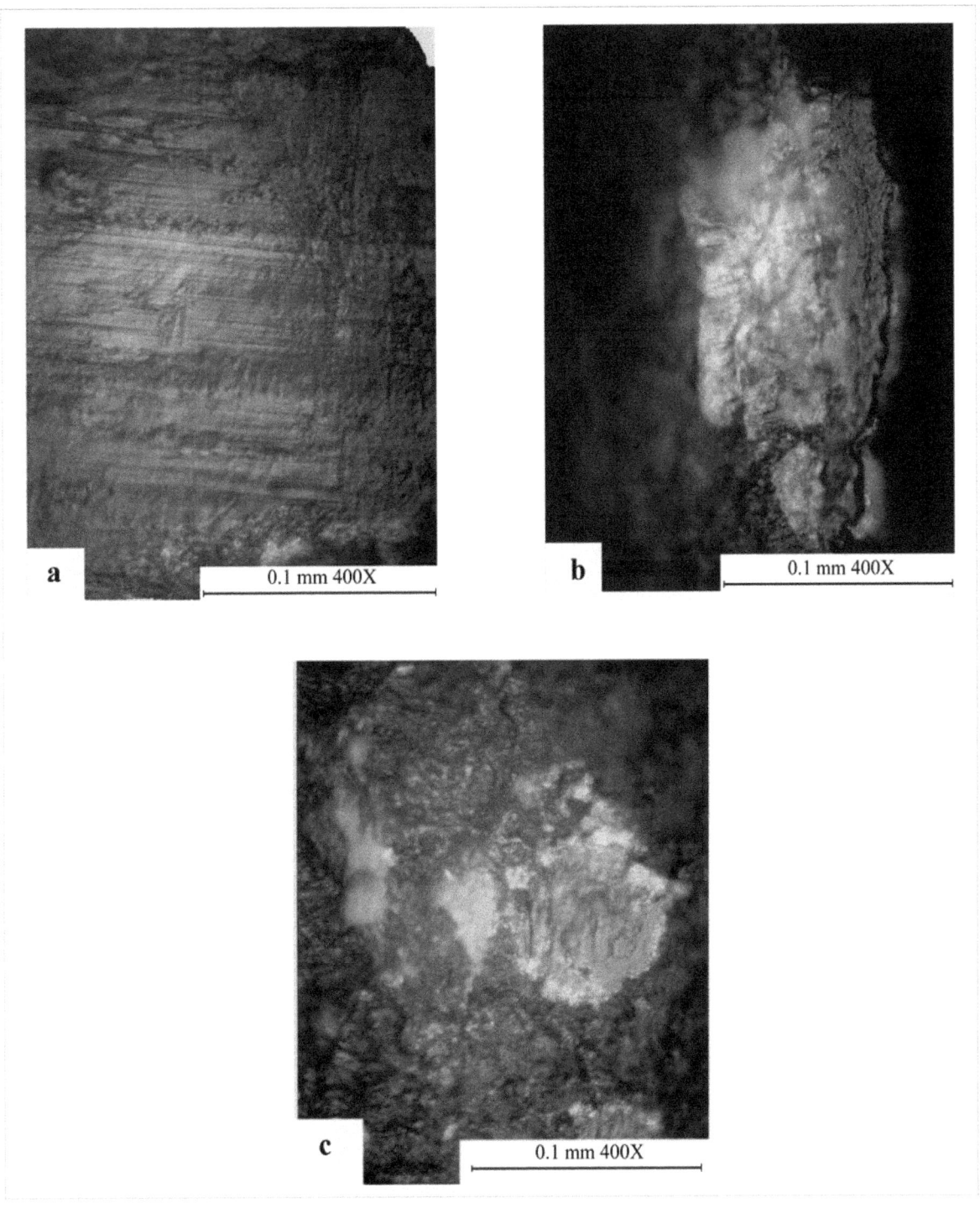

Appendix B-10*: a) WEB43B@400X – antler work; b) WEB46C@400X – bird butchery; c) WEB45A@400X – pumpkin processing.*

REFERENCES CITED

Akoshima, K., and G.C. Frison (1996). Lithic Microwear Studies of the Mill Iron Site Tools. In *The Mill Iron Site*, edited by George C. Frison, pp. 71–86. Univeristy of New Mexico Press, Albuquerque.

Andrefsky, W., Jr. (1991). Inferring Trends in Prehistoric Settlement Behavior from Lithic Production Technology in the Southern Plains. *North American Archaeology* 12: 129–144.

Andrefsky, W., Jr. (1994).The Geological Occurrence of Lithic Material and Stone Tool Production Strategies. *Geoarchaeology: An International Journal* 9:375–391.

Argant, J. (2002). Analyse pollinique. In *Solutre: 1968–1998*, edited by J. Combier and A. Montet-White, pp. 165–168. Mémoire 30, Société Préhistorique Française, Paris.

Banks, W.E. (1997). Solutré, Bloc P16: Investigation of Tool Technology and Tool Use with Analyses of Breakage Patterns. Paper presented at the 62nd Annual SAA Meeting, Nashville, Tennessee.

Banks, W.E. (1999). A Casting Method Suitable for High-Power Microwear Analysis. *Current Research in the Pleistocene* 16:105–107.

Banks, W.E. (2002a). Analyse tracéologique de l'outillage aurignacien (secteur M12). In *Solutré: 1968–1998*, edited by J. Combier and A. Montet-White, pp. 243–246. Mémoire 30. Société Préhistorique Française, Paris.

Banks, W.E. (2002b). A High-Power Use-Wear Analysis of Stone Tools Recovered from 14DO417. *Current Archaeology in Kansas* 3:14–20.

Banks, W.E., and M. Kay (2003). High-Resolution Casts for Lithic Use-Wear Analysis. *Lithic Technology* 28:27–34.

Barton, C. M., D.I. Olszewski, and N.R. Coinman (1996). Beyond the Graver: Reconsidering Burin Function. *Journal of Field Archaeology* 23:111–125.

de Beaulieu, J. L., and M. Reille (1984). A Long Upper-Pleistocene Pollen Record from Les Echets Near Lyon, France. *Boreas* 13:111–132.

de Beaulieu, J. L., and M. Reille (1989). The transition from temperate phases to stadials in the long Upper Pleistocene sequence from Les Echets. *Palaeogeography, Palaeoclimatology, Palaeoecology* 72:147–159.

Beyries, S. (1981). Etude De Traces D'utilisation Sur Des Empreintes En Latex. *Bulletin de la Société Préhistorique Française* 78(7):198–199.

Bienenfeld, P. (1995). Duplicating Archaeological Microwear Polishes with Epoxy Casts. *Lithic Technology* 20:29–39.

Binford, L.R. (1973). Interassemblage Variability—the Mousterian and the "Functional" Argument. In *The Explanation of Culture Change: Models in Prehistory*, edited by C. Renfrew, pp. 227–254. Duckworth, London.

Binford, L.R. (1977). Forty-seven Trips: A Case Study in the Character of Archaeological Formation Processes. In *Stone Tools as Cultural Markers: Change, Evolution and Complexity*, edited by R. V Wright, pp.24–36. Australian Institute of Aboriginal Studies, Canberra.

Binford, L.R. (1979). Organization and Formation Processes: Looking at Curated Technologies. *Journal of Anthropological Research* 35:255–273.

Binford, L.R. (1980). Willow Smoke and Dogs' Tails: Hunter-gatherer Settlement Systems and Archaeological Site Formation. *American Antiquity* 45:1–17.

Binford, L.R. (1982). Objectivity–Explanation–Archaeology–1981. In *Theory and Explanation in Archaeology*, edited by C. Renfrew, M. J. Rowlands, and B. A. Segraves, pp. 125–138. Academic Press, New York.

Binford, L.R. (1983). General Introduction. In *Working at Archaeology*, pp. 31–39. Academic Press, New York. Originally published in *For Theory Building in Archaeology: Essays on Faunal Remains, Aquatic Resources, Spatial Analysis, and Systemic Modeling*, edited by Lewis R. Binford, pp. 1–13, 1977. Academic Press, New York.

Bleed, P. (1986). The Optimal Design of Hunting Weapons: Maintainability or Reliability. *American Antiquity* 51:737–747.

Bordes, F. (1967). Considérations sur la Typologie et les Techniques dans le Paléolithique. *Quartaer* 18:25–55.

Bosselin, B. and F. Djindjian (1988). Un essai de structuration du Magdalénien français à partir de l'outillage lithique. *Bulletin de la Société Préhistorique Française* 85:304–331.

Bousman, C.B. (1993). Hunter-Gatherer Adaptations, Economic Risk and Tool Design. *Lithic Technology* 18:59–86.

Brink, J. (1978). The Role of Abrasives in the Formation of Lithic Use-Wear. *Journal of Archaeological Science* 5:363–371.

Burke, A. (1993). Applied Skeletochronology: The Horse as Human Prey During the Pleniglacial in Southwestern France. In, *Hunting and Animal Exploitation in the Late Paleolithic and Mesolithic of Eurasia*, edited by G. L. Peterkin, H. M. Bricker, and P. A. Mellars, pp. 145–150. Archaeological Papers of the American Anthropological Association, Number 4.

Combier, J. (1955). Les fouilles de 1907 à 1925. Mise au point stratigraphique et typologique. In *Solutré*, edited by M. Thoral, R. Riquet, and J. Combier, pp. 93–224. Nouvelle Séries No. 2. Travaux du Lavoratoire de Géologie de la Faculté des Sciences de Lyon.

Combier, J. (1976). Solutré. In *IX Congrès de l'Union Internationale des Sciences Préhistoriques et Protohistoriques, Livret-Guide de l'Excursion A*, Bassin du Rhône Paléolithique et Néolithique*, edited by Jean Combier and J. Thevenot, pp. 111–117. U.I.S.P.P., Paris.

Combier, J. (2002a). Solutré, site témoin des origines de l'archéologie préhistorique. In *Solutré: 1968–1998*, edited by J. Combier and A. Montet-White, pp. 17–26. Mémoire 30, Société Préhistorique Française, Paris.

Combier, J. (2002b). Les amas d'ossements magdaléniens secteurs N16 et P16: Les Décapages. In *Solutré: 1968–1998*, edited by J. Combier and A. Montet-White, pp. 99–110. Mémoire 30, Société Préhistorique Française, Paris.

Combier, J. (2002c). Les sondages: stratigraphy. In *Solutré: 1968–1998*, edited by J. Combier and A. Montet-White, pp. 65–77. Mémoire 30, Société Préhistorique Française, Paris.

Combier, J. (2002d). Le problème des déplacements humains, le territoire des chasseurs de Solutré. In *Solutré: 1968–1998*, edited by J. Combier and A. Montet-White, pp. 247–252. Mémoire 30, Société Préhistorique Française, Paris.

Combier, J., and J.L. Hofman (2002). Le secteur J10, le "magma" Gravettien. In *Solutré: 1968–1998*, edited by J. Combier and A. Montet-White, pp. 89–98. Mémoire 30, Société Préhistorique Française, Paris.

Combier, J., and A. Montet-White (2002a). Les secteurs L13 et M12, fouilles des niveaux du Paléolithique supérieur ancien. In *Solutré: 1968–1998*, edited by J. Combier and A. Montet-White, pp. 79–87. Mémoire 30, Société Préhistorique Française, Paris.

Combier, J., and A. Montet-White (2002b). Conclusion. In *Solutré: 1968–1998*, edited by J. Combier and A. Montet-White, pp. 267–274. Mémoire 30, Société Préhistorique Française, Paris.

Cook, J., and J. Dumont (1987). The development and application of microwear analysis since 1964. In *The human uses of flint and chert: Proceedings of the fourth international flint symposium held at Brighton Polytechnic 10–15 April, 1983*, edited by G. De G. Sieveking, and M.H. Newcomer, pp. 53–62. Cambridge University Press, New York.

Crabtree, D., and E. Davis (1968). Experimental Manufacture of Wooden Implements With Tools of Flaked Stone. *Science* 159:426–428.

Curwen, E.C. (1930). Prehistoric Flint Sickles. *Antiquity* 4:179–186.

Damblon, F., P. Haesaerts, and J. van der Plicht (1996). New datings and considerations on the chronology of Upper Paleolithic sites in the great Eurasiatic plain. *Préhistoire Européenne* 9:177–231.

Donner, J. (1975). Pollen Composition of the Abri Pataud Sediments. In, *Excavation of the Abri Pataud*, edited by H. Movius, pp. 160–173. American School of Prehistoric Research Bulletin No. 30. Peabody Museum, Harvard University, Cambridge, Massachusetts.

Enloe, J.G. (1993). Subsistence Organization in the Early Upper Paleolithic: Reindeer Hunters of the Abri du Flageolet, Couche V. In, *Before Lascaux: The Complex Record of the Early Upper Paleolithic*, edited by H. Knecht, A. Pike-Tay, and R. White, pp. 101–115. CRC Press, Boca Raton.

Enloe, J.G. (2000a). Le Magdalénien du Bassin parisien au Tardilgaciaire: la chasse aux rennes compare à celle d'autres espèces. *Mémoire de la Société Préhistorique Française* 28:39–45.

Enloe, J.G. (2000b). Chasse au cheval dans le Bassin parisien. *La Recherche* 332:20–22.

Evans, J. (1897). *Ancient stone implements, weapons, and ornaments of Great Britain*. 2nd ed. Longmans, Green, London.

Farrand, W.R. (1975). Analysis of the Abri Pataud Sediments. In, *Excavations of the Abri Pataud, Les Eyzies (Dordogne)*, edited by H. L. Movius, pp. 27–68. American School of Prehistoric Research Bulletin 30. Peabody Museum Press, Cambridge, Massachusetts.

Frison, G.C. (1968). A Functional Analysis of Certain Chipped Stone Tools. *American Antiquity* 33(2):149–155.

Geneste, J.-M., and H. Plisson (1993). Hunting Technologies and Human Behavior: Lithic Analysis of Solutrean Shouldered points. In, *Before Lascaux: The Complex Record of the Early Upper Paleolithic*, edited by H. Knecht, A. Pike-Tay, and R. White, pp. 117–135. CRC Press, Boca Raton.

Gonzalez-Urquijo, J. Emilio, and J.J. Ibanez-Estevez (2003). The Quantification of Use-Wear Polish Using Image Analysis: First Results. *Journal of Archaeological Science* 30:481–489.

Gould, R.A. (1980). *Living Archaeology*. Cambridge University Press, Cambridge.

Gould, R.A., D.A. Koster, and A.H. Sontz (1971). The Lithic Assemblage of the Western Desert Aborigines of Australia. *Antiquity* 36:149–169.

Grace, R. (1993). New Methods in Use-Wear Analysis. In *Traces et Foncion: Les Gestes Retrouvés*, edited by P. Anderson, S. Beyries, M. Otte, and H. Plisson, pp. 385–387. ERAUL No. 50. Liège.

Grace, R. (1996). Use-wear Analysis: The State of the Art. *Archaeometry* 38:209–229.

Grace, R., I.D. Graham, and M.H. Newcomer (1987). Preliminary investigation into the quantification of wear traces on flint tools. In *The human uses of flint and chert: Proceedings of the fourth international flint symposium held at Brighton Polytechnic 10–15 April, 1983*, edited by G. De G. Sieveking, and M.H. Newcomer, pp. 63–70. Cambridge University Press, New York.

Guiot, J. (1987). Late Quaternary Climatic Change in France Estimated from Multivariate Pollen Time Series. *Quaternary Research* 28:100–118.

Haesaerts, P., and B. Bastin (1977). Chronostratigraphie de la fin de la dernière glaciation à la lumière des résultats de l'étude lithostratigraphique et palynologique du site de Maisières-Canal (Belgique). *Géobios* 10:123–127.

Haesarts, P., and J. de Heinzelin (1979). *Le site paléolithique de Maisières-Canal*. Dissertationes Archaeologicae Gandenses 19. Brugge.

Hardy, B.L., M. Kay, A.E. Marks, and K. Monigal (2001). Stone Tool Function at the Paleolithic site of Starosele and Buran Kaya III, Crimea: Behavioral Implications. *Proceedings of the National Academy of Sciences* 98:1972–10977.

Henry, D.O., J.J. White, J. Beaver, S. Kadowaki, A. Nowell, H. Ekstrom, R. Dean, M. Gregg, M. Harrower, J. McCorriston, and S. Mussadeh (2001). *Excavation of Ain Abu Nekheileh: Report of 2001 Field Season*. Report to the Department of Antiquities of Jordan, pp. 1–8. Amman.

Hilton, M.R. (2003). Quantifying Postdepositional Redistribution of the Archaeological Record Produced by Freeze–Thaw and Other Mechanisms: An Experimental Approach. *Journal of Archaeological Method and Theory* 10:165–202.

Hoffman, R., and L. Gross (1970). Reflected-Light Differential-Interference Microscopy: Principles, Use and Image Interpretation. *Journal of Microscopy* 91:149–172.

Hofman, J.L., and A. Montet-White (1998). Solutré. Rapport de fouilles inédit. Manuscript available from the Musée de Préhistoire de Solutré (Saône-et-Loire), France.

Holley, G.A., and T.A. Del Bene (1981). An Evaluation of Keeley's Microwear Approach. *Journal of Archaeological Science* 8:337–352.

Howard, C.D. (1999). Amorphous Silica, Soil Solutions, and Archaeological Flint Gloss. *North American Archaeologist* 20:209–215.

Hurcombe, L. (1988). Some criticisms and suggestions in response to Newcomer et al. (1986). *Journal of Archaeological Science* 15:1–10.

Jeannet, M. (2002). Microfaune et environnement au Crot du Charnier à Solutré. In *Solutré: 1968–1998*, edited by J. Combier and A. Montet-White, pp. 169–180. Mémoire 30, Société Préhistorique Française, Paris.

Kantman, S. (1971). Essai sur le Problème de la Retouche d'utilisation dans l'étude du Matériel Lithique: Premiers Résultats. *Bulletin de la Société Préhistorique Française* 68:200–204.

Kay, M. (1996). Microwear Analysis of Some Clovis and Experimental Chipped Stone Tools. In, *Stone Tools: Theoretical Insights into Human Prehistory*, edited by G.H. Odell, pp. 315–344. Plenum Press, New York.

Kay, M. (1997). Imprints of ancient tool use at Monte Verde. In, *Monte Verde: A Late Pleistocene Settlement in Chile. Volume II: The Archaeological Findings*, edited by T.E. Dillehay, pp. 649–660. Smithsonian Institution Press, Washington, DC.

Kay, M. (1998). Scratchin' the Surface: Stone Artifact Microwear Evaluation. In, *Wilson-Leonard An 11,000-year Archeological Record of Hunter-Gatherers in Central Texas, Volume III: Artifacts and Special Artifact Studies*, edited by M.B. Collins, pp. 744–794. Studies in Archeology 31, Texas Archeological Research Laboratory, The University of Texas at Austin.

Kay, M. (2000). Use-Wear Analysis. In *The 1999 Excavations at the Big Eddy Site (23CE426)*, edited by N.H. Lopinot, J.H. Ray, and M.D. Conner, pp. 177–220. Special Publication No. 3. Center for Archeological Research, Southwest Missouri State University, Springfield.

Kay, M., and R. Solecki (2000). Pilot Study of Burin Use-Wear From Shanidar Cave, Iraq. *Lithic Technology* 25:30–41.

Keeley, L.H. (1974a). The Methodology of Microwear Analysis: A Comment On Nance. *American Antiquity* 39(1):126–128.

Keeley, L.H. (1974b). Technique and Methodology in Microwear Studies: A Critical Review. *World Archaeology* 5(3):323–336.

Keeley, L.H. (1978). Microwear Polishes on Flint: Some Experimental Results. In *Lithics and Subsistence: The Analysis of Stone Tool Use in Prehistoric Economies*, edited by Dave D. Davis, pp. 163–178. Publications in Anthropology, No.20. Vanderbilt University, Nashville,TN.

Keeley, L.H. (1980). *Experimental Determination of Stone Tool Uses: A Microwear Analysis*. University of Chicago Press, Chicago.

Keeley, L.H. (1981). Reply to Holley and Del Bene. *Journal of Archaeological Science* 8:348–352.

Keeley, L.H. and Newcomer, M.H. (1977). Microwear analysis of experimental flint tools: a test case. *Journal of Archaeological Science* 4:29–62.

Keller, C. (1966). The Development of Edge-Damage Patterns On Stone Tools. *Man* 1:501–511.

Kervazo, B., and S. Konik (2002). Etude géologique du gisement de Solutré. In *Solutré: 1968–1998*, edited by J. Combier and A. Montet-White, pp. 135–154. Mémoire 30, Société Préhistorique Française, Paris.

Klima, B. (1995). Dolni Vestonice II: Ein Mummutjägerrastplatz und seine Bestattungen. *The Dolni Vestonice Studies 3, ERAUL 73*.

Knecht, H. (1988). *Upper Paleolithic Burins: Type, Form, and Function. BAR International Series 434*. Oxford.

Knudson, R. (1979). Inference and Imposition in Lithic Analysis. In *Lithic Use-Wear Analysis*, edited by B. Hayden, pp. 269–282. Academic Press, New York.

Knutsson, K., and R. Hope (1984). The Application of Acetate Peels in Lithic Usewear Analysis. *Archaeometry* 26(1):49–61.

Kuhn, S.L. (1994). A Formal Approach to the Design and Assembly of Mobile Toolkits. *American Antiquity* 59:426–442.

Laville, H. (1988). Recent developments on the Chronostratigraphy of the Paleolithic in the Périgord. In, *Upper Pleistocene Prehistory of Western Eurasia*, edited by H.L. Dibble and A. Montet-White, pp. 147–160. University Museum Monograph 54. The University Museum, University of Pennsylvania. Philadelphia.

Leroi-Gourhan, A. (1964). *Le Geste et la Parole 1: Technique et langage*. Albin Michel, Paris.

Leroi-Gourhan, Arl. (1968). L'Abri du Facteur à Tursac (Dordogne): Analyse pollinique. *Gallia Préhistoire* 11(1):123–131.

Leroi-Gourhan, Arl. (1997). Chauds et Froids de 60,000 a 15,000 BP. *Bulletin de la Société Préhistorique Française* 94:151–160.

Leroi-Gourhan, Arl., and M. Girard (1979). Analyses Polliniques de la Grotte de Lascaux. In *Lascaux Inconnu: XII supplement a Gallia Prehistoire*, edited by Arl Leroi-Gourhan, and J. Allain, pp. 75–80. CNRS, Paris.

Levine, M. (1983). Mortality Models and the Interpretation of Horse Population Structure. In *Hunter-Gatherer Economy in Prehistory*, edited by G. Bailey, pp. 23–57. University of Cambridge Press, Cambridge.

Levi Sala, I. (1986). Use Wear and Post-Depostional Surface Modification: A Word of Caution. *Journal of Archaeological Science* 13:229–244.

Moir, J.R. (1914). The Striation of Flint Surfaces. *Man* 90:177–182.

Montet-White, A. (2002a). Les outillages des chasseurs de Solutré. In *Solutré: 1968–1998*, edited by J. Combier and A. Montet-White, pp. 225–241. Mémoire 30, Société Préhistorique Française, Paris.

Montet-White, A. (2002b). Les amas d'ossements magdaléniens secteurs N16 et P16: Répartition Spatiale de l'Industrie Lithique. In *Solutré: 1968–1998*, edited by J. Combier and A. Montet-White, pp. 110–111. Mémoire 30, Société Préhistorique Française, Paris.

Montet-White, A., and J. Combier (2002). Les amas d'ossements magdaléniens secteurs N16 et P16: Conclusions. In *Solutré: 1968–1998*, edited by J. Combier and A. Montet-White, pp. 115–116. Mémoire 30, Société Préhistorique Française, Paris.

Montet-White, A., J. Evin, and T. Stafford (2002). Les Datations Radiocarbone des AMAS Osseux de Solutré. In *Solutré: 1968–1998*, edited by J. Combier and A. Montet-White, pp. 181–189. Mémoire 30, Société Préhistorique Française, Paris.

Mortillet, G. (1888). Les sepultures de Solutré. *Bulletin de la Société d'Anthropologie de Lyon.* April 14:70–75.

Moss, E.H. (1983). *The Functional Analysis of Flint Implements: Pincevent and Pont d'Ambon, Two Case Studies from the French Final Paleolithic*, vol. 177. BAR International Series, Oxford.

Moss, E.H. (1997). Lithic Use-Wear Analysis. In *Klithi: Paleolithic settlement and Quaternary Landscapes in northwest Greece*, Volume 1: *Excavation and intra-site analysis at Klithi*, edited by Geoff Bailey, pp. 193–205. McDonald Institute for Archaeological Research, University of Cambridge.

Munaut, A.V. (1984). L'Homme et son Environnement Végétal. In, *Peuples chasseurs de la Belgique préhistorique dans leur cadre naturel*, edited by D. Cahen and P. Haesaerts, pp. 59–66. Mémoires de l'Institut Royal des Sciences Naturelles 171. Bruxelles.

Newcomer, M.H., and L.H. Keeley (1979). Testing a Method of Microwear Analysis with Experimental Flint Tools. In *Lithic Use-Wear Analysis*, edited by Brian Hayden, pp. 195–206. Academic Press, New York.

Newcomer, M., R. Grace, and R. Unger-Hamilton (1986). Investigating Microwear Polishes With Blind Tests. *Journal of Archaeological Science* 13:203–217.

Nilsson, S. (1838). *Skandinaviska Nordens Urinvanare.* Lund: Berlingska Boktryckeriet. (English edition: 1843). *The Primitive Inhabitants of Scandinavia.* 1868. London).

Odell, G.H. (1975). Micro-Wear in Perspective: A Sympathetic Response to Lawrence H. Keeley. *World Archaeology* 7:226–240.

Odell, G.H. (1978). Préliminaires d'une analyse fonctionnelle des points microlithiques de Berfumermeer (Pays-Bas). *Bulletin de la Société Préhistorique Française* 75:37–49.

Odell, G.H. (1981). The Morphological Express At Function Junction: Searching for Meaning in Lithic Tool Types. *Journal of Anthropological Research* 37(4):319–342.

Odell, G.H. (2001). Stone Tool Research at the End of the Millennium: Classification, Function, and Behavior. *Journal of Archaeological Research* 9:45–100.

Odell, G.H., and F. Odell-Vereecken (1980). Verifying the Reliability of Lithic Use-Wear Assessments By "Blind Test": The Low Power Approach. *Journal of Field Archaeology* 7:87–120.

Olausson, D. (1980). Starting from Scratch: The History of Edge-Wear Research from 1838 to 1978. *Lithic Technology* 9:48–60.

Olsen, S. (1989). Solutré: A Theoretical Approach to the Reconstruction of Upper Paleolithic Hunting Strategies. *Journal of Human Evolution* 18:295–327.

Olsen, S. (1995). Pleistocene Horse-Hunting at Solutré: Why Bison Jump Analogies Fail. In *Ancient Peoples and Landscapes*, edited by E. Johnson, pp. 65–75. Museum of Texas Tech University, Lubbock.

Paquereau, M.-M. (1978). Flores et climats du Würm III dans le Sud-Ouest de la France. *Quaternaria* 20:123–164.

Pautrat, Y., and D. Pugh (2002). Les Alentours du Gisement: Le Site Mousterien de Solutré-Village. In, *Solutré: 1968–1998*, edited by J. Combier and A. Montet-White. Société Préhistorique Française, (in press).

Petraglia, M., D. Knepper, P. Glumac, M. Newman, and C. Sussman (1996). Immunological and Microwear Analysis of Chipped-stone Artifacts from Piedmont Contexts. *American Antiquity* 61:127–135.

Pike-Tay, A., and H.M. Bricker (1993). Hunting in the Gravettian: An Examination of Evidence from Southwestern France. In, *Hunting and Animal Exploitation in the Late Paleolithic and Mesolithic of Eurasia*. Number 4 ed., edited by G.L. Peterkin, H.M. Bricker, and P. Mellars, pp. 127–143. Archaeological Papers of the American Anthropological Association.

Plew, M.G., and J.C. Woods (1985). Observation of Edge Damage and Technological Effects on Pressure Flaked Stone Tools. In *Stone Tool Analysis: Essays in Honor of Don E. Crabtree*, edited by M.G. Plew, J.C. Woods, and M.G. Pavesic, pp. 211–227. University of New Mexico Press, Albuquerque.

Plisson, H. (1983). An Application of Casting Techniques for Observing and Recording of Microwear. *Lithic Technology* 12:17–21.

Prost, D.-C. (1993). Nouveaux Termes pour une Description Microscopique des Retouches et Autres Enlèvements. *Bulletin de la Société Préhistorique Française* 90(3):190–195.

Ranere, A.J. (1975). Toolmaking and tool use among the preceramic peoples of Panama. In *Lithic Technology*, edited by E.H. Swanson, Jr., pp. 173–209. Mouton, The Haque.

Reille, M., and J.L. de Beaulieu (1988). History of the Wurm and Holocene Vegetation in Western Velay (Massif Central, France): A Comparison of Pollen Analysis from Three Corings At Lac Du Bouchet. *Review of Palaeobotany and Palynology* 54:233–248.

Reille, M., and J.L. de Beaulieu (1990). La Fin De L'Eemien Et Les Interstades Du Prewurm Mis Pour La Premiere Fois En Evidence Dans Le Massif Central Francais Par L'annalyse Pollinique. *Comptes-Rendus de l'Academie des Sciences* 306 (II):1205–1210.

Rose, J.J. (1983). A Replication Technique for Scanning Electron Microscopy: Applications for Anthropologists. *American Journal of Physical Anthropology* 62:255–261.

Sackett, J.R. (1966). Quantitative Analysis of Upper Paleolithic Stone Tools. *American Anthropologist* 68:356–394.

Schlanger, N. (1990). Techniques as Human Action: Two Perspectives. *Archaeological Review from Cambridge* 9:18–26.

Schlanger, N. (1994). Mindful technology: unleashing the chaîne opératoire for an archaeology of mind. In *The ancient mind: elements of cognitive archaeology*, edited by C. Renfrew and E. Zubrow, pp. 143–151. Cambridge University Press, Cambridge.

Sehested, N.F.B. (1884). *Praktiske forsøg. Archaeologiske Undersøgelser* 1878–1881:1–40.

Sellami, F. (2002). La dynamique des sols colluviaux et son impact sur les assemblages anthropiques du site de Solutré. In *Solutré: 1968–1998*, edited by J. Combier and A. Montet-White, pp. 155–164. Mémoire 30, Société Préhistorique Française, Paris.

Sellet, F. (1993). Chaîne Opératoire: The Concept and Its Applications. *Lithic Technology* 18:106–112.

Semenov, S.A. (1964). *Prehistoric Technology*. Cory, Adams, and Mackay, London.

Semenov, S.A. (1970). The Form and Functions of the Oldest Stone Tools (a Reply to Prof. Bordes). *Quatar* 21:1–20.

Shott, M. (1986). Technological Organization and Settlement Mobility: An Ethnographic Examination. *Journal of Anthropological Research* 42:15–51.

Shott, M. (1989). On Tool-Class Use Lives and the Formation of Archaeological Assemblages. *American Antiquity* 54:9–30.

Smith, P.E.L. (1966). *Le Solutréen En France*. Publications de l'Institut de Préhistoire de l'Université de Bordeaux, Mémoire No. 5.

Sokal, R.R., and F.J. Rohlf (1995). *Biometry: The Principles and Practice of Statistics in Biological Research* (3rd Edition). W.H. Freeman and Company, New York.

Sonnenfeld, J. (1962). Interpreting the Function of Primitive Implements. *American Antiquity* 28:56–65.

Spurrell, F.C.J. (1884). On Some Paleolithic Knapping Tools and Modes of Using Them. *Journal of the Royal Anthropological Institute* 13:109–118.

Stemp, W.J., and M. Stemp (2003). Documenting Stages of Polish Development on Experimantal Stone Tools: Surface Characterization by Fractal Geometry Using

UBM Laser Profilometry. *Journal of Archaeological Science* 30:287–296.

Straus, L.G. (1988). The Uppermost Pleistocene in Gascony. In, *Upper Pleistocene Prehistory of Western Eurasia*, edited by H.L. Dibble, and A. Montet-White, pp. 41–60. The University Museum, University of Pennsylvania, Philadelphia.

Straus, L.G. (1996). The Archaeology of the Pleistocene-Holocene Transition in Southwest Europe. In, *Humans at the End of the Ice Age: The Archaeology of the Pleistocene-Holocene Transition*, edited by L.G. Straus, B.V. Eriksen, J.M. Erlandson, and D.V. Yesner, pp. 83–99. Plenum Press, New York.

Svoboda, J. (1990). Moravia during the Upper Pleniglacial. In, *The World at 18000 BP: High Latitudes*, Volume 1, edited by O. Soffer and C. Gamble, pp. 193–203. Unwin Hyman, London.

Svoboda, J., and H. Svoboda (1985). Les industries de type Hohunice dans leur cadre stratigraphique et écologique. *L'Anthropologie* 89:505–514.

Symens, N. (1986). A Functional Analysis of Selected Stone Artifacts from the Magdalenian Site at Verberie, France. *Journal of Field Archaeology* 13:213–222.

Teaford, M.F., and O.J. Oyen (1989). Live Primates and Dental Replication: New Problems and New Techniques. *American Journal of Physical Anthropology* 80:73–81.

Thomas, D.H. (1986). *Refiguring Anthropology: First Principles of Probability & Statistics* (2nd Edition). Waveland Press, Prospect Heights, Illinois.

Tringham, R., G. Cooper, G. Odell, B. Voytek, and A. Whitman (1974). Experimentation in the Formation of Edge Damage: A New Approach to Lithic Analysis. *Journal of Field Archaeology* 1(1,2):171–196.

Turner, E. (2002). Les amas d'ossements magdaléniens secteurs N16 et P16: Répartition Spatiale des Restes de Faune. In *Solutré: 1968–1998*, edited by J. Combier and A. Montet-White, pp. 111–115. Mémoire 30, Société Préhistorique Française, Paris.

Ungar, P.S. (1994). Incisor Microwear of Sumatran Anthropoid Primates. *American Journal of Physical Anthropology* 94:339–363.

Unger-Hamilton, R. (1989). Analyse expérimentale des microtraces d'usure: Quelques controversies actuelles. *l'Anthropologie* 93:659–672.

Van der Hammen, T., T.A. Wijmstra, and W. van der Molen (1965). Palynological study of a very thick peat section in Greece and the Wurm glacial vegetation in the Mediterranean region. *Geologica Mijnbouw* 44:37–39.

Vaughan, P.C. (1985). *Use-wear Analysis of Flaked Stone Tools*. University of Arizona Press, Tucson.

Vaughan, P.C. (1990). Use-Wear Analysis of Mesolithic Chipped-Stone Artifacts from Franchthi Cave. In *Les Industries lithiques taillées de Franchthi (Argolide, Grèce): Les Industries du Mésolithique et du Néolithique Initial* (Volume II), edited by Catherine Perlès, pp. 239–253. Indiana University Press, Bloomington and Indianapolis.

Vayson, A. (1922). L'etude Des Outillages En Pierre. *L'Anthropologie* 32(1):1–38.

Warren, S.H. (1914). The Experimental Investigation of Flint Fracture and Its Application to Problems of Human Implements. *Journal of the Royal Anthropological Institute* 44:412–450.

Weissmüller, W. (1997). Eine Korrelation der d18O-Ereignisse des grönländischen Festlandeises mit den Interstadialen des atlantischen und des Kontinentalen Europa im Zeitraum von 45 bis 14 ka. *Quartär* 47-48:89–112.

Weniger, G.-C. (1990). Germany at 18,000 B.P. In *The World at 18,000 BP: High Latitudes*, vol. 1, edited by O. Soffer, and C. Gamble, pp. 171–192. Unwin Hyman, Boston.

White, L.A. (1940). The Symbol: The Origin and Basis of Human Behavior. *Philosophy of Science* 7:451–463.

Wijmstra, T.A. (1969). Palynology of the first 30 meters of a 120 m deep section in northern Macedonia. *Acta Botan. Neerl.* 18:511–527.

Wilmsen, E.N. (1968). Functional Analysis of Flaked Stone Artifacts. *American Antiquity* 33(2):156–161.

Woillard, G. (1978). Grande Pile Peat Bog: A Continuous Pollen Record for the Last 140,000 Years. *Quaternary Research* 9:1–21.

Woillard, G., and W. Mook (1982). Carbon-14 Dates At the Grande Pile: Correlation of Land and Sea Chronologies. *Science* 215:159–161.

www.ingramcontent.com/pod-product-compliance
Ingram Content Group UK Ltd.
Pitfield, Milton Keynes, MK11 3LW, UK
UKHW061213180426
11947UKWH00029B/2023